HOW M*AGNETS* can SAVE YOUR LIFE

MOSES DURAZO

I humbly dedicate this book to the memory of my revered mentor, Dr. Isaac Goiz Durán, M.D., the brilliant founder of *Medical Pair Biomagnetism*. His invaluable contributions to the medical field and holistic wellness were immeasurable, and his unwavering commitment to treating each person as a whole inspired and propelled me on this mission.

Table of Content

Disclaimer

The author, editor and publisher do not accept any responsibility for any consequences from application of the information in this book and make no warranty, expressed or implied, with respect to the contents of this book. Consult a doctor if you're injured or if you suffer from any medical conditions. This publication presents only the author's opinions which are based on their knowledge, experiences and beliefs. The techniques and theories offered here do not represent a scientific consensus or prevention or self-help. Results will be based on an individual's specific situation and will vary for everyone. You use all information and techniques published in this book at your own risk and based on the power of your free will.

Preface

If your life is burdened by pain and suffering and you have exhausted all possible avenues, I offer a beacon of hope. Drawing from the extensive research of pioneers in my holistic healthcare field, and my further adaptation of it, combined with my personal experience, I'm certain I hold two of the most significant health secrets of all time.

Maybe your physician hasn't mentioned this to you, given that it's not universally known within conventional allopathic medical practice; I'm referring to the transformative potential of Goizean Medical Pair Biomagnetism therapy (or the Biomagnetic Pair Theory) and of my own methodology called Recalibration Biomagnetism.

As a certified practitioner, Medical Pair Biomagnetism therapy forms the cornerstone of my practice. It's a complimentary science-based theory that allows me to help prevent, pH-diagnose and treat an array of ailments with pairs of medium-intensity magnets.

These magnets, specifically used to regulate an organism's pH levels, bring about a profound shift. Disruptions in the pH levels of organs or body systems are linked with harmful intruders such as viruses, toxins, parasites, fungi, and the like.

"Magnets?" you may ask surprised upon learning about my specialty. However, when I tell my story and people submit themselves to this therapy; skepticism often gives way to amazement. This field of biomagnetic therapy came into my life in 2008 and transformed me forever.

A chronic digestive issue that tormented me for over four years vanished overnight following a single session. I had tried everything; I mean I graduated from the university with holistic medicine training, and sought help from other healthcare practitioners, but the agony was relentless – then, it was suddenly over!

Over the years, I've gone deeper into this incredible field, enhancing my knowledge and contributing to the treasure trove of discoveries already made. More notably, I've developed my own revolutionary six-day biomagnetic *recalibration methodology* using magnets, detailed in my bestselling book, *Biomagnetism: The Mind, Body, Spirit Recalibration System*. This system can be your starting point to tackling many health issues discussed in this comprehensive, holistic guide, imparting well-rounded knowledge about this domain of care.

The medical biomagnetic pair therapy was initially discovered and developed by the late Dr. Isaac Goiz Duran of Mexico as a means of restoring wellness by correcting pH distortions leading to homeostasis without a single medicine or the need for surgery. Today, it has won accolades from hundreds of thousands worldwide who've personally experienced its benefits, united in their praise.

Imagine the dramatic reduction in pain, suffering, and exorbitant healthcare costs if everyone on the planet were to try this biomagnetic medicine method. I continue to encourage all healthcare consumers to actively write and call their insurance providers, demanding the inclusion of Biomagnetism in their benefits package. Change doesn't just happen on its own; we must all participate in creating a better healthcare system for each other. My hope is that, together with you, we may persuade the governments and insurers of the world to recognize this powerful holistic healthcare practice and cover it. I make an argument for this in my book, *Medical Magnets: Saving Lives and Millions of Dollars in Healthcare – Why Your Insurance Plan should Pay for Medical Biomagnetism.*

Don't let pain deprive you of your life's quality. Reclaim the beauty and vitality of optimal living by embracing a health perspective rooted in nature and nature's forces.

Of course, Biomagnetism alone, or any other modality for that matter, can't prevent and treat pain and suffering. They must be coupled with a holistic lifestyle approach and sound choices in other life aspects.

For example, attempting to cure liver cirrhosis while persisting with alcohol or any other harmful substance abuse is an exercise in futility. If you want to achieve true well-being, it's essential to let go of destructive habits and embrace a healthier lifestyle.

Mental well-being cannot be attained if you constantly and purposefully hold grudges and engage in conflicts. To experience inner peace and emotional balance, it's necessary to cultivate an attitude of opportunities to be found in difficult situations, which can lead us to forgiveness, understanding, and harmonious relationships with others.

Similarly, if your goal is weight loss, relying solely on a diet while regularly consuming highly processed foods or leading a sedentary lifestyle is highly unlikely to yield sustainable results.

However, both Medical Biomagnetism and Recalibration Biomagnetism can assist you in managing present health issues, pains and behaviors that impede your journey towards optimal living, and it can serve as the catalyst for long-term, healthy change.

This book has been crafted with the following objectives:

1. To inspire conscious living and facilitate a shift from detrimental habits, enabling you to experience optimal well-being and tranquility.

2. To familiarize you with Medical Pair Biomagnetism and the basic underlying science of how and why it works.

3. Encourage the application of Recalibration Biomagnetism in your personal health journey, emphasizing its accessibility and effectiveness.

4. Equip you with the knowledge and resources needed to have magnets on hand, emphasizing their importance in Medical Pair Biomagnetism and Recalibration Biomagnetism therapy.

5. Highlight the global reach and potential benefits of Medical Pair Biomagnetism through our services like the *BiomagScan* (personalized illustrations) or *Distance Healing*, asserting that geographical boundaries are no hindrance to harnessing the power of this therapy.

Since the release of the book's first edition in 2013, I've been moved by the countless testimonials from readers whose lives have significantly improved. It's becoming increasingly evident how impactful the combination of conscious living for better lifestyle habits and Biomagnetism can be for our personal health and that of humanity as a whole.

Chapter 1

An Empowered Life with Recalibration Biomagnetism

"Your vision will become clear only when you can look into your own heart. Who looks outside, dreams; who looks inside, awakes."

– CARL JUNG

In 2013, a gentleman stumbled upon one of my numerous videos on YouTube and took the initiative to call me. He applauded my contributions to the field of Medical Pair Biomagnetism. Despite our first encounter, our conversation was filled with warmth and laughter as though we'd known each other for years.

He made an insightful comment, "You know something Moses, when we're young we're out there chasing riches looking to make lots of money. When we get older, money doesn't matter anymore, because now we're looking for good health and to live as long as possible."

I've heard lots of people say similar things many times. It's not uncommon to hear people expressing a desire to trade their wealth for a return to youthful vigor and health.

Cultivate your own wealth of health

In essence, this book is about wealth creation. Not the conventional monetary wealth, but the richness of leading your unique version of an ideal life, brimming with energy and health.

And who gets to define this perfect life? You do.

It's all about understanding your health and existence, and living with a sense of purpose – essentially, gaining control over your life.

If your ambitions also include material wealth, rest assured, this book can guide you towards that goal, because when you're in good health and have a clear focus, you have the power to accomplish anything.

Yet, reaching your goals can prove elusive if you're constantly battling pain on a mental, physical, and spiritual level.

If you've sought help in all forms, from therapy to surgery, medications, natural remedies, diverse therapies, or even exploring various religious avenues, and still found no relief, the resultant frustration can be overwhelming.

If all you can manage is temporary pain management through potentially harmful pharmaceutical, let me assure you – there are better, safer, longer lasting ways!

Over the years, numerous individuals have utilized the skills and solutions I've learned and discovered, converting their pain and discomfort into inner peace, equilibrium, and a profound understanding of their existence on the mind, body, and spirit planes.

I firmly believe that these solutions can benefit you as well, but the first step must be yours. Progress doesn't happen without initiative.

I've had the privilege of studying and collaborating with the staff at the University of California (UC) Santa Cruz, UC Irvine, UC San Francisco, Children's Hospital of Los Angeles, Dr. Goiz' Medical Biomagnetism Research Center, and two different Alphabiotic Associations. Each educational venture provided invaluable insights into the universal human struggles and how different ways of healing and educational tools try to solve them.

My two-decade-long journey of research and study has led me to the realization that there are more effective methods to alleviate pain and suffering than those offered by conventional pharma-based healthcare. My life's work is centered around empowering individuals to achieve self-sufficiency by providing them with easily accessible strategies derived from nature. Through my efforts, I aim to make Medical Biomagnetism and Recalibration Biomagnetism readily available, enabling people to regain control over their lives. Ultimately, my goal is to guide others in living purpose-driven lives, because ultimately, purpose is what keeps us focused on thoughts and actions that benefit every aspect of our lives.

Discover the transformative power of mind, body, spirit recalibration

In my life-enhancing book, *Biomagnetism: The Mind, Body, Spirit Recalibration System*, I unveil the remarkable method that allows you to embrace ongoing recalibration while embracing life's ever-shifting nature. The biomagnetic recalibration method is applicable regardless of your age, current health status, medications, supplements, treatments, or health habits.

If you're interested in embarking on this self-care journey, I invite you to explore our Biomagnetic Recalibration kits, complete with therapeutic magnets, available at *www.SaveMeMagnets.com* and Amazon. Taking control of your life means designing your own path instead of simply letting circumstances dictate your journey. In other words, it's about reclaiming your power by dissolving the barriers standing in your way!

Each and every one of us deserves to wake up every day with a sense of purpose and enthusiasm for our work and responsibilities. When we open ourselves to receiving the ever-present abundance all around us, that my friends, is the epitome of true wealth. It's entirely possible to live a joyful life when we understand ourselves and the profound healing methods that guide us towards our desired destination.

This book here in your hands serves as a guide to self-discovery and reaching your utmost potential through action! As we journey through life, we continuously add new chapters to our personal book. Some of these chapters are filled with love and joy, while others are marked by anxiety and even tragedy. Regrettably, many people find their pages filled with mundane routines and unfulfilling experiences, lacking a clear sense of direction or meaningful goals. They allow life to unfold without purpose, as if merely going through the motions driven by doubt and worry.

Pause for a moment and ask yourself this pivotal question: *"Am I content, at peace and appreciative with my past, present, and does my current lifestyle support the dreams and visions I have for tomorrow?"* This question holds immense significance, as each day shapes our future. What are you actively working towards?

If you're determined to revolutionize your life, it becomes crucial to visualize your ideal future, especially in the face of life's inevitable challenges. It's essential to deeply understand what success truly means to you, transcending external influences. Envision yourself in your perfect tomorrow – how does it feel? Do you feel energized and healthy? Do you possess an unwavering trust in yourself and the journey ahead? Are you committed, loyal, and honorable in your pursuits?

Once you have identified your virtues and desires, the path to achieving them becomes accessible by setting milestones and ardently striving to reach them. It's a process that requires dedication, perseverance, and unwavering focus. As you embark on this transformative journey, move beyond the mere desire to alleviate pain and envision a life that is truly fulfilling, where your primary focus is nurturing your overall well-being.

By recognizing and embracing your core values, passions, and aspirations, you create a blueprint for a purpose-driven life. Embrace each milestone as a stepping stone towards your vision of success, and let your virtues guide your actions. Remember, this journey is not merely about achieving external accomplishments; it's about aligning your thoughts, actions, and choices with your authentic self.

With each milestone reached and every challenge overcome, you inch closer to the vibrant and fulfilling life you envisioned. Embrace the process of growth and transformation, and trust in your innate ability to navigate through life's twists and turns. As you nurture your well-being and embody your chosen virtues, you will gradually forge a path that leads to a life of purpose, joy, and profound fulfillment.

Think about the age at which you last felt physically, emotionally, and spiritually strong. Now, complete this statement: *I'm ___ years old, and my mind, body, and spirit are strong and in perfect harmony!* Now that you've identified one of the happiest times of your life, strive to live that way every single day and in every moment. Remind yourself of this empowering declaration each morning upon awakening and especially during times of stress and frustration.

You may find that your present responsibilities far surpass those of your perfect past, and you may have endured profound tragedies that deeply impacted you. However, tapping into the joy of your perfect self can help you realign and continue the journey of transforming your life.

What if happiness has always eluded you? What if your life has never felt perfect? You're not alone. Some individuals lack joyful memories when everything felt right in their world, a truly disheartening circumstance. In such cases, I invite you to reflect upon a single special event that brought you immense joy. It could be a graduation, your first job, a memorable birthday celebration, a moment of first love, or a serene place where you found peace. Use this event or place as your touchstone, bringing you back to happiness and enabling you to envision your perfect future. I truly believe that when we focus on living with joy, that this will bring greater abundance to our lives.

Because challenges are always present, recognize that recalibrating your body and mind is a continuous journey – one that empowers you to live a purpose-driven life while embracing the ever-changing nature of existence.

Life is more than simply living without pain or disease

I firmly believe that life is meant to be a joyous celebration, filled with meaningful moments and deep connections with others, even in the face of life's inevitable challenges. From both our personal and the broader global challenges we encounter, opportunities emerge for personal growth, the cultivation of gratitude, and the receipt of blessings. These elements, in turn, infuse our lives with a deep sense of purpose and significance.

It's through the act of assuming meaningful responsibilities, making a positive impact on humanity as a whole, and achieving inner peace and balance within ourselves, that we discover the true essence of living with purpose. This journey toward purpose is a remarkable and fulfilling endeavor that enriches not only our own lives but also the lives of those we touch along the way. With this perspective in mind, consider the lasting impact you're creating, a legacy that will shape the path for future generations to come.

I'm here to help you embrace and celebrate life, and in the following pages, I'll guide you on this transformative journey. While the title suggests the role of magnets in enhancing your well-being, this book goes far beyond into the holistic realm of overall health and vitality. It embraces the idea that every facet of our lives is interconnected and offers insights into considering different aspects of life and taking action that can yield tremendous benefits on your own terms.

You don't need to feel frustrated or powerless when facing challenges. In fact, experiencing such emotions can have a detrimental effect on our overall health. But even during the most difficult times, there are valuable lessons to be learned. Once we assimilate these lessons, we can transcend the pain and return to living life optimally. When we genuinely understand that there are valuable lessons in every experience, our quality of life is enhanced. It allows us to understand our emotional intelligence, our actions or lack thereof that landed us in that situation. This understanding empowers us to avoid similar situations or confront them more constructively in the future. Therefore, I invite you to be present with your emotions but shift from frustration to empowerment. If you're complacent, most likely you're not growing…I encourage you to seek out constructive discomfort for your personal growth.

Going through life and making good choices for ourselves might seem difficult, but it's not impossible. We can learn how to make decisions that are best for us and our well-being. It just takes some practice and learning along the way. Remember, you have the power to make choices that will help you live a happy and fulfilling life. With the right guidance, and the right circle of friends, it can be a straightforward and empowering process. But where can one find such guidance amidst the myriad of conflicting information circulating in the world?

When thinking about this question, I'm reminded of a show featuring Dr. Mehmet Oz and two other doctors – a nutritionist and a cardiologist – who openly admitted that much of what they learned in medical school has since been proven wrong. In the realm of medical science, theories are constantly evolving as new facts and discoveries come to light. In today's post COVID pandemic era, it's crystal clear that a large portion of the global population can be easily misled to believe that experimental pharmaceutical products are both safe and effective. This misplaced trust has resulted in unnecessary pain, suffering and even loss of life, because of blind trust in authority figures (*the doctor is always right*), a deliberate disregard for potential risks (*it can't be that harmful; I've never experienced vaccine harm before*), or emotional pressure (*fear of job loss if the vaccine is not taken*).

It's essential to understand that no single field of medicine or study has all the answers for every health issue. Many people rely solely on conventional allopathic medicine, without realizing that it may not have all-encompassing solutions. It's crucial to recognize that knowledge is constantly growing and changing. Take, for instance, the case of the COVID vaccine. We were bombarded with the narrative that widespread vaccination would render us immune to the virus and make it vanish.

However, we know that this was not true – the vaccine did not prevent infection or transmission and has been associated with grave injury, including death. Despite this, some "experts" still argue that the benefits could outweigh the risks, a viewpoint with which I personally disagree with. It's important to recognize that there exist official and censored narratives within the medical community. Without a doubt, there's great value in exploring diverse perspectives and approaches, while critically evaluating the available data and facts. By doing so, we can make informed decisions that contribute to our well-being and ensure we stay up-to-date with the latest and truthful information in the field of healthcare.

It's essential to acknowledge that our healthcare system in the United States, like in many other places, is fraught with shortcomings. When comparing high-income countries, the US ranks highest or near-highest in terms of obesity, infant mortality, heart and lung disease, sexually transmitted infections, and injuries, according to the National Institutes of Health.

Consider this: in the pre-COVID-pandemic era, on a yearly basis, was conservatively estimated that 7,400 people die from medication errors, 12,000 from unnecessary surgeries, 20,000 from preventable errors in hospitals, 80,000 from hospital-acquired infections, and 106,000 from adverse drug effects (Campbell and Campbell, 2006). Each year, approximately 750,000 people are rushed to the emergency room due to adverse reactions to medication, and all of the above figures were estimated to get worse with the passing of time, and *current* data is showing that it has by a large percentage.

While medical doctors strive to provide the best possible care, they can only work with the knowledge they possess (or are *allowed* to acknowledge by their governing bodies), just as I can offer guidance based on what I know. Hence, it makes sense to consider natural medicine within the context of your life. There is no foolproof argument suggesting that healthcare solutions exclusively offered in the allopathic medical field are always the best for every individual. In fact, there is evidence to suggest that at times, they may simply not be effective, and even making the problem worse.

By exploring alternative approaches and considering a holistic perspective, we open ourselves to a wider range of possibilities and potential solutions. It's about embracing a comprehensive approach to well-being, one that takes into account the intricacies of our unique selves and recognizes the ever-evolving nature of all medical therapy knowledge (natural, technologically and pharmaceutically based).

You deserve to live optimally

You deserve to live your life to the fullest, taking control of your wellness and exploring various paths to optimal well-being. You deserve to experience a high quality of life, where you can potentially add extra years and maintain good health. Now let me ask you: *Do you wholeheartedly believe that you deserve an exceptional quality of life, regardless of past, present and future challenges?* It's understandable if you don't fully believe it yet, and this book will help you align yourself with that belief. I invite you to take the holistic steps for mind, body, and spirit to reach that 100%, because the truth is, you truly deserve it. Not only for yourself and your loved ones, but for the betterment of humanity as a whole!

As you hold this book in your hands, you possess the key to unlock your transformation and embark on the journey towards a life of fulfillment. It serves as a valuable resource and trusted guide, illuminating the path to infinite possibilities. However, it's important to remember that true transformation requires your active participation and willingness to take meaningful action.

These actions revolve around *Medical Biomagnetism, Recalibration Biomagnetism, Alphabiotic spinal alignments, nutrition, and emotional intelligence.* While two of these steps may require assistance from specialists, the rest are entirely within your control. The first step involves letting go of limiting mindsets and discovering your life's reset button. You must define your personal wellness goals, assess your physical, emotional, and spiritual challenges, and recognize your strengths in these areas.

In the upcoming chapters, I'll guide you on how to create the perfect life tailored to your needs and desires. It's a life that not only can but does exist. Together, we'll explore the limitless possibilities and empower you to embrace a life of vibrant well-being and fulfillment.

Chapter 2

Successful Steps to Optimal Living

"To change one's life, start immediately, do it flamboyantly, no exceptions."
– WILLIAM JAMES

To live a life of optimal quality, it's essential to understand and implement steps that can prevent, improve, and even heal illness and disease. Unfortunately, many individuals endure physical, emotional, and spiritual suffering every day. They have grown accustomed to pain, accepting it as an inevitable part of life and aging, rather than taking proactive measures to embrace a life free from pain and filled with joy. It's time to break free from this mindset and embark on a journey of holistic well-being.

Instead of addressing the root causes of their mind, body, spirit pain and seeking appropriate action, many individuals prefer to manage their suffering by masking it with medicines, supplements, drugs, alcohol, emotional eating, distractions like excessive television or work hours, and other temporary solutions. However, it would be more beneficial to cease playing the victim to our painful circumstances and take responsibility for the problems we often inadvertently create for ourselves.

To truly thrive and lead an optimal life, it's crucial to have an understanding of life itself and how our bodies function. Most importantly, we must grasp that we're responsible for a large percentage of what manifests in our lives, both the good and the bad.

Life encompasses a range of experiences – it involves living and dying, crying and laughing, working and resting, eating and digesting, thinking, sleeping, and dreaming. These are the daily events we all encounter. However, there are deeper influences that drive us, forces related to our quest for peace, balance, self-improvement, love, and genuine happiness.

In this book, we embark on a profound exploration of the driving forces that shape our lives. Our intention is to guide you towards a deep understanding of your true essence and equip you with the tools for transformative growth. Through the exploration of essential concepts and practical strategies, our aim is to empower you to live a life harmoniously aligned with your authentic self, where the repetitive patterns of pain and suffering no longer hold sway. This journey of self-discovery and self-improvement paves the way for you to find your rightful place of optimal well-being, where you actively address pain and embrace proactive solutions. Together, we embark on a transformative voyage towards a life abundant with joy, vitality, and lasting fulfillment.

Steps to Living an Optimal Life

1. **Know yourself to help yourself:** Developing self-awareness is crucial if you want to experience positive transformation and

live your best life. Identify your goals, aspirations, strengths, and weaknesses to gain a deeper understanding of yourself and work towards positive transformation. If you're open and interested in bioenergetic pendulum work, a potentially useful book to help you in this process is, *Spiritual Thriving: Pendulum Charts to Identify Blockages & Help Yourself Grow Spiritually*, by Victoria Vivaldi.

2. **Seek support and guidance:** Trust that those who love and honor you will support you through difficult times. Surround yourself with a supportive network of friends, family, or mentors who can provide guidance and encouragement along your journey.

3. **Embrace urgency and take action:** Imagine if you knew that the world was ending tomorrow. Use that perspective to motivate yourself to take action towards achieving your dreams and aspirations. Don't wait for the perfect moment – start taking steps now.

4. **Utilize Medical Pair Biomagnetism:** Explore the power of Medical Pair Biomagnetism, a therapeutic technique that involves placing magnets on specific points of the body to promote balance and wellness. Learn about its benefits, seek our healing service, and incorporate it into your health and well-being routine. With technology, we can help guide you even if you're on the other side of the world (visit *www. SaveMeMagnets.com*).

5. **Embrace Recalibration Biomagnetism:** Discover the transformative potential of Recalibration Biomagnetism, a method that utilizes introspection and the application of magnets to the body for six days to balance the body's

energy, help dissolve personal barriers, enhance intuition and problem solving, be called to action, and enhance overall well-being. This is a self-care process that anybody can submit themselves to that does not require professional help; however, guidance does exist (visit *www.SaveMeMagnets.com* for more information).

6. **Visualize your perfect life:** Take time to envision your ideal life in detail. Consider the various aspects that would bring you fulfillment and happiness. Visualize yourself living that life and use this vision as a guide for making choices and taking actions aligned with your aspirations.

7. **Reflect on strengths and weaknesses:** Reflect on your personal strengths and weaknesses and consider how they can be harnessed to bridge the gap between your current reality and your ideal life. Leverage your strengths to overcome challenges and capitalize on opportunities for growth.

8. **Continual learning and growth:** Commit to lifelong learning and personal growth. Stay open to new experiences, explore different perspectives, and seek knowledge and skills that will support your journey towards optimal living. Take one of our on-demand courses on self-care biomagnetism (visit *www.SaveMeMagnets.com*), or take a course at your local community college today.

9. **Practice gratitude and let go of what no longer serves you:** Cultivate a gratitude mindset by appreciating the blessings in your life. Let go of limiting beliefs, negative patterns, and past traumas that hold you back. Embrace the lessons pain and suffering yield, and find peace with the past to create space for new possibilities.

10. **Take aligned action:** Put your plans into action by setting clear goals and taking consistent steps towards achieving them. Break down big goals into smaller, manageable tasks and celebrate each milestone along the way.

Remember that personal growth is a continuous process, and these steps can serve as a guide for your journey; adapt them to your own needs and circumstances, and be open to exploring additional strategies and practices that resonate with you. By following these steps and incorporating Medical Pair Biomagnetism and Recalibration Biomagnetism, and so much more, I'm going to deliver in this book, you can unlock your full potential and live a life of optimal well-being.

Chapter 3

Setting Up A System That Works For You

"When you have balance in your life, work becomes an entirely different experience. There is a passion that moves you to a whole new level of fulfillment and gratitude, and that's when you can do your best…for yourself and for others."

– CARA DELEVINGNE

Designing a personalized system for success involves considering various dimensions of life that contribute to overall well-being and fulfillment. In this chapter, we'll explore how your life system can positively impact 13 dimensions of life, while also highlighting the benefits of incorporating Medical Pair Biomagnetism (MPB) and Recalibration Biomagnetism (RB). Additionally, I'll introduce the 6-day challenge as a transformative opportunity within your personalized system.

1. **Physical Fitness:** Your personalized system can include exercise habits that promote physical fitness. Engaging in regular physical activity not only improves your physical

well-being but also boosts energy levels, enhances mood, and reduces the risk of chronic diseases. MPB and RB may help support your body's natural healing processes and restore balance to enhance physical fitness.

2. **Nutritional Health:** Consider how your personalized system addresses nutritional health. By making conscious choices about the things you ingest, you can support optimal functioning of your body. Explore the benefits of incorporating a balanced diet, and MPB and RB in order to contribute to better nutrient absorption and overall nutritional well-being.

3. **Logical/Intellectual Fitness:** Your personalized system can include ongoing learning and intellectual growth. Emphasize the importance of continuous education to enhance logical thinking and expand knowledge. MPB and RB can support mental clarity and focus.

4. **Emotional Intelligence:** Incorporate practices into your system that develop emotional intelligence, focusing on developing awareness, empathy, and effective regulation of feelings. These are key elements of this dimension. Both MPB and, more specifically, RB can facilitate emotional healing and provide support in managing emotions, thereby enhancing your capacity for emotional intelligence.

5. **The Neighbor:** Consider how your personalized system influences your relationships with others. Focus on being present, practicing active listening, and cultivating empathy. MPB and RB may foster emotional well-being, which

positively impacts your interactions and connections with others.

6. **Spirituality:** Reflect on the dimension of spirituality within your personalized system. Explore practices that align with your beliefs and values, providing meaning and purpose in your life. MPB and RB may contribute to spiritual growth and awareness.

7. **Love Relationship:** Within your personalized system, if appropriate to your life, nurture a harmonious and fulfilling love relationship. Emphasize effective communication, emotional intimacy, and shared values. MPB and RB can support healing and balance within intimate relationships.

8. **Parenting:** Consider how your personalized system supports your role as a parent, guardian, or role model to children. Incorporate strategies for fostering positive parenting practices and nurturing the well-being of your children, or the children in your life and community. MPB and RB may enhance your mind, body, spirit ability to provide a supportive and loving environment for your children.

9. **Ancestry:** Explore how your personalized system honors the legacy of your parents and ancestors. Consider incorporating family traditions and values that connect generations. RB can assist in healing ancestral patterns and promoting generational well-being.

10. **Social Life:** Within your personalized system, place importance on cultivating meaningful friendships and social connections. Prioritize quality interactions, engaging in

activities that foster positive relationships. MPB and RB contribute to emotional balance and social well-being.

11. **Money Beliefs:** Evaluate your relationship with money and how it aligns with your personalized system. Develop healthy money beliefs and practices that support financial well-being. MPB and RB can assist in releasing limiting beliefs and blocks related to money, allowing for a healthier and more abundant mindset.

12. **Career:** Consider how your personalized system aligns with your career aspirations and professional growth. Set goals and take action steps to pursue a fulfilling and meaningful career. MPB and RB can support your clarity, focus, and alignment in career-related decisions.

13. **Quality of Life:** Reflect on what you truly deserve in life and how your personalized system contributes to your overall quality of life. Prioritize self-care, set boundaries, and engage in activities that bring joy and fulfillment. MPB and RB can support your overall well-being and enhance your experience of life.

Participation in the 6-Day Challenge

Within your personalized system, consider submitting yourself to the transformative 6-day biomagnetic recalibration process in conjunction with MPB. This process provides an opportunity to recalibrate your mind, body, and spirit, promoting balance, healing, and alignment. You may engage in the 6-day challenge to amplify the benefits of your personalized system and accelerate your journey towards success and well-being (more info at *www.SaveMeMagnets.com*).

Designing a personalized system for success involves addressing the 13 dimensions of life and incorporating practices that support growth and fulfillment in each area. By exploring the potential of MPB and RB within your system, you can further enhance the benefits and results. Embrace the 6-day recalibration process as a transformative opportunity to accelerate your progress and create a life of holistic well-being and success. Remember, your personalized system is a dynamic and evolving framework that empowers you to navigate through life with intention and purpose.

Chapter 4

Navigating Stress: Understanding and Managing Its Impact

"Tension is who you think you should be. Relaxation is who you are."
– CHINESE PROVERB

S tress is an ever-present aspect of our lives, whether we consciously acknowledge it or not. But what does it truly mean to be stressed? Is stress harmful, or does it serve a purpose? Can we realistically avoid stress altogether? In this chapter, we'll explore the complex nature of stress, its potential consequences, and most importantly, how we can effectively manage and mitigate its impact on our lives.

The Stress Response: When faced with stress, our bodies respond by releasing regulating hormones and neurotransmitters. These chemicals initiate a heightened state of alertness, a natural and healthy response that helps us navigate challenging situations and perceive potential threats. Imagine a scenario where we felt no stress in the face of danger; we might neglect taking necessary precautions to protect ourselves, potentially leading to harm or becoming victims of attacks.

Consequences of Chronic Stress: While acute stress responses are adaptive, living with constant stress, fear, worry, and anxiety can prevent our bodies from returning to a state of inner balance. Over time, this chronic stress can disrupt the harmony within our glandular, nervous, and metabolic systems. Failure to address and manage stress effectively can result in a cascade of imbalances, impacting our overall mind, body, spirit well-being and functioning.

Managing Stress through Lifestyle Choices: Recognizing that stress is an inevitable part of life, our focus should shift towards managing stress rather than attempting to avoid it entirely. Stress can stem from various sources, including demands, relationships, work and educational-related pressures, money, environmental factors, our dietary choices, and more. By understanding the sources of stress and their effects on our well-being, we can proactively take effective steps to overcome these challenges and promote stress management in our daily lives.

The Power of Sleep and Rest: Undeniably, sleep and rest play a crucial role in managing stress. Engaging in restful sleep allows our bodies to replenish energy, enhance cognitive function, and support emotional well-being. Unfortunately, many individuals are deprived of quality sleep due to racing thoughts and worries about work, finances, relationships, health, and other concerns. Additionally, the demands of modern life, such as long work hours, multiple jobs, and excessive activities, coupled with the responsibilities of raising a family and dealing with traffic, can contribute to an unhealthy, unsatisfying, low-energy, and frustrated lifestyle. It's essential to recognize that regardless of material wealth, if burdened by stress, we may truly live in poverty.

Stresses from Various Angles: In our modern world, stressors surround us from virtually every angle. Even the food we consume can impact our stress load. Following the wisdom of Hippocrates, the father of medicine, we must acknowledge that everything we ingest has a direct effect on our physical, mental, and spiritual functioning. While in our youth, we may not immediately notice the impact of consuming genetically modified organisms (GMOs), foods high in sugar, refined products, pesticides, and nutrient-deficient additives, with age, our bodies prematurely deteriorate. An imbalanced, low-nutrient diet further exhausts our glandular system and exacerbates or leads to poor health conditions.

Food and Medicine (Potential Harms): Food, which should serve as nourishment, can also become a source of harm. Similarly, the medicines we take to cure us can have unintended consequences. Often, when prescribed medication, we receive a list of possible side effects from our pharmacist. However, without exploring potential lifestyle changes, such as improvements in nutrition and exercise, we frequently opt for medication without considering alternatives. Pharmaceutical medicine, though it may offer short-term relief, can be detrimental in both the short and long term. Many individuals have reported feeling better after discontinuing prescribed medication due to frustration with its effects. However, even though people understand that their condition isn't improving and may even worsen with medication, they often struggle to let go of it due to lingering fears instilled by physicians. The belief that taking medication is the only path to avoiding dire consequences like death, stroke, or heart attacks persists. Yet, the reality remains that people on medication still experience these life-threatening events on a daily basis.

Environmental Factors and Stress: In addition to internal factors, external environmental toxins also contribute to our stress levels. Although we may not visibly perceive them, we are constantly exposed to pollution in the air, such as the byproducts from cars and factories worldwide. Moreover, everyday construction materials like carpets, floors, walls, ceilings, roofs, and cabinets contain numerous chemicals that can harm our well-being. It's advisable to ventilate our living spaces by opening doors and windows regularly, especially after installing new materials, to release trapped vapors. Furthermore, using air purifiers in our bedrooms, where we spend a significant amount of time sleeping, can greatly improve air quality. Even the water from our faucets may contain bleach, fluoride, and other unknown toxins, emphasizing the importance of cooking with clean water, as boiling alone does not eliminate these harmful substances. Our bodies were not designed to withstand the constant onslaught of environmental toxins that permeate our daily lives, adding excessive burden to our overall well-being.

Stress from Microbes: Microbes, both inside and outside our bodies, play a significant role in our stress levels and overall health. Astonishingly, bacterial cells outnumber the cells that make up our organism, highlighting their prevalence. While not all bacteria cause harm – in fact, the ones that make up our microbiome are part of our well-being – microbes have metabolic processes that involve excretion of waste inside us. In a healthy and balanced organism, these toxins are efficiently processed and eliminated without our awareness. However, in an unbalanced and diseased body, a wide range of symptoms can arise, including fatigue, fever, back pain, headaches, inflammation, digestive problems, organ and glandular failure, and many more. Understanding these challenges led to the creation of a simple yet effective biomagnetic detoxification boosting protocol using three magnets. Detailed instructions for this tool can be found in my book, *Biomagnetism: The Mind, Body, Spirit Recalibration System*, which offers a means to alleviate stress from our bodies.

Other Sources of Stress: Beyond internal and external factors, various aspects of our lives can contribute to stress. Relationships, initially intended to provide support, can become sources of stress in certain circumstances. Instead of fostering our growth, family, friends, and colleagues may undermine our efforts and diminish our well-being. It's essential not to point fingers and blame others when faced with such situations. Rather, we must recognize our own role in participating in unhealthy interactions that contribute to stressful relationships. Taking responsibility for our own behavior is key to minimizing stress in our relational dynamics. Additionally, physical stress resulting from work, accidents, falls, fractures, overexertion in sports, or lack of exercise can significantly impact our stress load. It's evident that stress can arise from various aspects of our lives, challenging and influencing our mind, body, and spirit.

The Endocrine System and Stress: Throughout centuries, ancient Taoists recognized the significance of the seven glands within the endocrine system in regulating energy flow among different body systems. Each gland possesses a specific role in affecting our entire organism, interconnected and working in harmony. These glands do not function independently; instead, they are intricately linked through the circulatory system. Chemical substances, akin to energy, flow through our bloodstream, maintaining a biochemical balance necessary for the proper functioning of our bodies. Modern endocrinology echoes the wisdom of the ancient Taoists, confirming that glands produce hormones (chemical substances/energy) that flow through the bloodstream, reaching all tissues of the body and directly influencing various mind-body-spirit functions. If one gland within the endocrine system malfunctions, the other glands compensate by increasing their energy output, aiming to restore balance within the system. While scientific advancements have allowed us to understand the specific chemical names and responsibilities of these glands, the fundamental principle remains the same – the endocrine system auto-regulates in response to hyper- or hypo-secretion of hormones.

In conclusion, stress is an inescapable part of life, but through understanding and effective management, its impact can be minimized. By recognizing the physiological and psychological mechanisms of the stress response, acknowledging the consequences of chronic stress, and embracing lifestyle choices that promote stress management, we can regain control over our well-being. Prioritizing the power of sleep, adopting holistic nutrition practices, critically evaluating the role of medication, addressing environmental factors, understanding the impact of microbes, fostering healthy relationships, and taking care of our physical well-being with biomagnetic strategies are essential steps in this journey. Finally, the intricate workings of the endocrine system remind us that our actions and choices impact multiple aspects of our lives. By nurturing our body's energy flow and maintaining balance within this system, we can cultivate resilience and enhance our overall well-being.

Chapter 5

Embracing Pain to
Create a Better Life

'The single overriding objective in wellness is creating constant personal renewal where we recognize and act on the truth that each day is a miraculous gift and our job is to untie the ribbons. That's the Law of Esprit: living life with joy."

– GREG ANDERSON

Have you ever heard someone belittle emotional pain by dismissing it as insignificant? "It's *only* emotional." In reality, emotional suffering is a very real and debilitating experience that deserves our attention and understanding. Ignoring or downplaying our feelings can have serious consequences, impacting our overall well-being and even leading to violent tragedies. It's crucial that we self-evaluate and develop our *emotional intelligence* to overcome these challenges and focus on finding solutions.

Developing and enhancing emotional intelligence is key to navigating life's ups and downs. It empowers us to rise above petty problems and focus on creating meaningful solutions. The biomagnetic recalibration method addresses the importance of emotional intelligence and offers practical guidance for enhancing this vital aspect of our lives. The positive feedback I have received from users of this method affirms the relevance and effectiveness of this approach in our modern world.

As human beings, we have the capacity for both love and hatred, peace and violence, harmony and chaos. Emotional intelligence allows us to make conscious choices that align with love, peace, harmony, and success. However, life often presents us with obstacles that trigger emotions like hatred, violence, and chaos. By nurturing our emotional intelligence, we gain the tools to navigate through these challenges without losing ourselves in harmful thoughts and actions.

According to Dr. Ryke Geerd Hamer, a pioneer in the field of New German Medicine, no illness, except for poisoning, occurs without an emotional shock. This means that our emotional well-being plays a significant role in our physical health. Emotional shocks can manifest as physical symptoms like cold extremities, high blood pressure, poor appetite, weight loss, or sleep disturbances. It's important to recognize the connection between our emotional experiences and their impact on our overall well-being.

Sometimes, we carry emotional wounds from past traumatic experiences that continue to affect us subconsciously. To initiate the healing process, we must identify and make peace with these deep-rooted emotions. By reflecting on our past and acknowledging the traumatic events that have shaped us, we can release the harm they have caused and find inner peace. The journey towards emotional healing begins with self-evaluation and a willingness to confront and let go of painful memories.

It's never too late to release the painful memories of our past. When we take the courageous step to let go, we open ourselves to the many wonderful qualities and experiences that life has to offer. Everything we have ever lived is stored within us, and even if we're not actively thinking about past events, our subconscious mind continues to carry their influence. By self-evaluating and addressing the stored pain within us, we can transform our lives and become healthier and happier individuals.

Continuing to live with pain is a choice that affects not only ourselves but also those around us. It dampens our spirit, dreams, and goals and has a direct impact on our relationships and interactions with others. Overcoming our painful experiences leads to personal growth, wisdom, and the ability to pass on valuable lessons to future generations. By choosing to radiate peace, love, and forgiveness, we contribute to a more harmonious world.

Losing a loved one is one of the most challenging experiences we can face. It's essential to honor the grieving process, but eventually, we must transform our grief into gratitude for the special moments we shared with the departed. Although it may seem difficult, finding gratitude behind the pain is crucial for healing and moving forward. Accepting the reality of death and letting go of fear allows us to embrace peace and open ourselves to miraculous healing.

To create an optimal life, we must honor the vision of self-improvement and growth that our ancestors had when they brought us into this world. This requires us to change our actions, thoughts, and behaviors. By acknowledging our role in relationships, examining our habits, and fostering peace within ourselves, we can overcome pain and experience a transformative healing process. Our actions shape our reality, and by choosing positive change, we can create a brighter future.

Healing emotional wounds is not an easy journey, but it's one worth taking. By recognizing the lessons hidden within our pain, we gain wisdom, strength, and the ability to contribute positively to the world. Fear and anger only perpetuate the disease process, while peace, love, and acceptance pave the way to healing. As we let go of the past and choose a path of self-improvement and emotional well-being, we discover the power within ourselves to create a life filled with joy, harmony, and personal fulfillment.

Chapter 6

Three Empowering Strategies
for Emotional Freedom

*"Sometimes, you have to let it go, just to see if
there's anything worth holding onto."*

- JOHN GREEN

In this chapter, we'll explore three powerful strategies that you can perform all by yourself that can help you overcome challenges and achieve emotional freedom. These strategies will assist you in restoring balance, peace, and wellness to your life. It's important to recognize that even seemingly insignificant problems can cause imbalance and affect our peace of mind. Let's explore these strategies and discover their transformative potential.

Strategy 1: Venting for Liberation

This powerful exercise involves venting out load, and we suggest making it a top priority. Find a location in nature, such as the ocean, a forest, or a park, where you can freely express your emotions without self-censoring. Get barefooted, and really connect with the ground. While conducting this exercise, it's important to remember that any ill-wishes or comments towards others are a part of the process of liberating yourself from negative emotions, so don't hold back; cursing and crying are all very common responses.

Keep in mind that the primary goal here is to release all the negativity that you've been holding onto. By purging yourself of pain and negative emotions, you take significant steps toward uncovering hidden lessons that are waiting to be discovered or gaining a deeper understanding of life-enriching insights. It's worth noting that individuals who have undergone this process for the first time have reported that it typically took about an hour to complete. Subsequent venting sessions tend to be much shorter, as they revisit the process. Furthermore, many individuals have shared that the negative emotions they once harbored, such as hatred or regrets, were immediately replaced by a profound sense of peace and a newfound understanding of life.

During this exercise, even if they are not or have never been in your life, imagine speaking with the parent of your opposite sex – if you're male, visualize speaking to your mother; and if you're female, envision talking to your father. Even though you're not actually venting to your parent directly, this exercise may prove challenging for many individuals since open communication with the opposite-sex parent is not always prevalent. However, it's precisely this difficulty that makes the exercise so powerful. The goal is to purge your emotions as if you were confiding in them or expressing any deep-seated grievances.

Even if you believe you do not need this exercise, I encourage you to give it a try. Many individuals have found it to be an eye-opening experience, helping them become aware of and release emotional baggage they didn't realize they were carrying from as long ago as childhood. Venting can bring clarity to your feelings, improve your direction in life, enhance your relationships, and even alleviate physical pain in some cases. Make it a priority to engage in this exercise and discover its potential for emotional healing.

Strategy 2: Your Advice for Solutions

The second strategy involves asking yourself a crucial question that can lead to solutions and breakthroughs. This exercise originated from my personal experience with an eye infection that caused immense frustration. On the second night of grappling with this frustration, I asked myself, *If someone sought my advice for the same problem, what would I tell them?*

Remarkably, this question triggered immediate thoughts of a natural eye-drop recipe I had known for many years. I realized that my fixation on the problem had prevented me from considering potential solutions. When we detach ourselves from our issues and adopt an external perspective, the answers become clearer.

Now, I invite you to take a moment to identify any challenge in your life and step back from it. Imagine that someone close to you, whether it's your children, best friend or a loved one, is going through the same challenge. Ask yourself what advice or guidance you would give them. It's common that we provide valuable and compassionate advice to others while we struggle to apply the same wisdom to ourselves.

By applying this perspective to all of life's obstacles, no matter their size or significance, you can gain valuable insights and discover solutions that may extend beyond your immediate struggles. The goal here is not necessarily to have profound epiphanies or to solve all of humanity's problems with this question. Instead, it's about expediting your transformation process. You can revisit this question later in the day, tomorrow, and in the days that follow. Each time you do, you may find that new thoughts and actions emerge, contributing to your proactive healing journey.

In addition to the above strategies, consider activities like playing music, singing, participating in religious or cultural rituals, painting or drawing, journaling, writing letters or poetry, exercising, creating memory books, photography, cooking, joining support groups, and more. The key is to give your pain a voice, allowing yourself to heal and find liberation.

Living with unresolved pain, loss, grief, or resentment diminishes our life experience. Taking responsibility for our feelings and actively seeking solutions is crucial to our emotional well-being. By accepting and acknowledging our challenges while actively working towards positive change, we distinguish between a life consumed by emotional suffering and stagnation, and a life filled with growth and fulfillment.

Strategy 3: Unlocking Solutions During Sleep

Thomas Edison intelligently said, "Never go to sleep without a request to your subconscious." The third strategy that helps in overcoming emotional problems and finding solutions is the realm of dreams. Our dream function gives us the remarkable ability to gain insights, guidance, and resolutions to the challenges we face in our waking lives.

During sleep, our conscious mind takes a backseat, allowing our subconscious to wander freely. Dreams are not merely idle nighttime adventures; they hold the potential to provide profound guidance and solutions. It's within this realm that the *Doubling Time Theory*, proposed by Dr. Jean-Pierre Garnier Malet, sheds light on the potential of dreams as problem-solving mechanisms. According to Dr. Garnier, our dreams connect us to a part of ourselves that operates beyond the constraints of time and space.

When we consciously set our intentions before sleep, we can tap into this powerful problem-solving function. Just as I discovered during my personal journey, posing a question or seeking guidance in our dreams can lead to profound insights and solutions. By describing our challenges and questions in detail before sleep, we allow our intuitive faculties to process and analyze the infinite possibilities.

You may find that your dreams become more vivid and filled with symbolism that upon awakening don't make sense, and that's fine. What matters is that within our cells, we have a new memory of positive actions to take. Dr. Garnier puts it simply, that our responsibility to ourselves is to live following our gut feeling fully trusting that our actions are the absolute correct ones.

It's essential to acknowledge that this approach requires an open mind and trust in your decision making and action taking abilities. Trust yourself to guide you towards healing and resolution. As you integrate the practices of venting, tuning into your best advice, and embracing the insights from your dreams, you can enhance your overall well-being.

As we conclude this chapter, I urge you to embrace the strategies and exercises presented here. By incorporating these practices into your life, you can overcome challenges, achieve emotional freedom, and lead a more fulfilling existence. Remember that the power to transform your life lies in your hands. Choose to appreciate and celebrate every aspect of life, including its challenges, as they can serve as catalysts for personal growth and a renewed sense of well-being.

Chapter 7

Unlocking the Power of Biomagnetic Science for Optimal Wellness

"Success is to wake up each morning and consciously decide that today will be the best day of your life."

– KEN POIROT

As you continue your journey towards enhanced consciousness and implementing the practices from the previous chapters, a profound transformation is underway in your life. You may already be experiencing its effects, even if you haven't fully recognized them yet.

In this chapter, I want to deliver to you valuable information that has the potential to not only change your life but also save it. It has certainly saved mine, and that's why I'm deeply passionate about pioneering the field of biomagnetic-pair science.

But before we explore this topic, it's crucial to ensure that you have laid the right philosophical foundation for your life. Living an optimal quality of life depends on cultivating the right mindset. Let's quickly recap key points:

1. First and foremost, value and trust yourself to make the right decisions.

2. Identify the perfect age inside of you and start living in alignment with that ideal version of yourself.

3. Release unnecessary emotional baggage by venting out loud in nature.

4. Identify and address challenges by taking a step back and asking yourself what advice you would give to a loved one in a similar situation.

5. Harness the power of your dreams by posing questions and obtaining the solutions as you fall asleep.

6. Utilize the self-care Biomagnetic Recalibration method, which you can obtain at *www.SaveMeMagnets.com* or Amazon to support your overall healing.

By consciously living by design and incorporating these principles into your life, you can make a significant difference with the power of your mind, intentions, and actions.

Now, let's explore the field of biomagnetic science, which can take your wellness journey to a higher level that your mind alone cannot achieve.

Are you tired of being sick?

To fully grasp the concept of Medical Pair Biomagnetism (MPB) therapy, it's crucial to understand the problem it aims to solve. Many people, including you and your family, are tired of feeling sick and exhausted all the time. You might sleep, but still wake up fatigued, in pain, and frustrated. You find yourself annoyed with the world, questioning the purpose of life, and relying on pills to manage the pain. You eagerly wait for bedtime or seek distractions to forget about the obstacles affecting your life.

Unfortunately, many of us fall into the trap of false hope, as we're sold quick fixes and empty promises in the form of pharmaceuticals, minerals, vitamins, lotions, and potions. Regrettably, so many have been, and continue to be hurt by these products regardless of the safety claims. Unfortunately, the suffering is chronic and immense. Many don't see any other way out besides continuously managing the pain. In cases like these, true healing seems elusive. You might have made efforts to exercise more, improve your nutrition, and adopt healthier habits, yet something still feels off. I understand this struggle because I have experienced it myself.

At this point, you might feel that nothing can help you. You're not alone in this sentiment. Millions of people share your thoughts and feelings. I know this because I've been there too. I have lived with chronic pain in mind, body, and spirit, and I understand the debilitating and frustrating nature of it. There were moments when I felt like I was losing a war within my own body.

However, everything changed in a matter of hours after my first biomagnetic session. I once lived with chronic digestive problems, trying various treatments over four years without finding lasting relief. But after just *one* 25-minute biomagnetic session, the problem completely disappeared. This is why I'm so passionate about MPB.

MPB: Not Just for Health Challenges

MPB offers hope and healing not only to those living with frustration and health challenges but also to healthy individuals. As more people witness the transformative results and testimonials of MPB therapy, they are realizing that Biomagnetism's objective is inner balance, which contributes to a richer, happier life by also preventing disease.

This is an essential point because we're often told to maintain a balanced diet and exercise for good health. While this is true, it's also true that even athletic and healthy individuals can fall ill and be diagnosed with conditions like cancer, arthritis, diabetes, heart failure, lupus, multiple sclerosis, and more. In fact, in very recent times, there are countless news reports of young healthy professional athletes suddenly dying all over the world. It's an ironic reality.

For those already diagnosed with debilitating conditions or those who may face such challenges in the future, MPB offers hope for overcoming these health issues. It may seem impossible or too good to be true, or you might dismiss it as medical quackery. But I urge you not to dismiss it without giving it a fair chance.

You'll never truly know what's possible until you try it for yourself. If I hadn't accidentally discovered MPB, I would still be living in misery, feeling worse as time went by. Countless individuals have expressed their regrets for waiting so long to try this therapy, as they experienced immediate pain relief and even complete cures.

The Origins of Medical Pair Biomagnetism

MPB is a healing method that utilizes natural magnets (without machines) to correct biochemical imbalances in the body. In essence, magnets are applied to help detect and restore proper pH balance; this is essential for healing. While magnets have been used for healing purposes for centuries, MPB was discovered relatively recently in 1988 by the late Dr. Isaac Goiz Durán, M.D. who was based in Mexico City.

Dr. Goiz's interest in therapeutic uses of magnetic fields stemmed from learning about Dr. Richard Broeringmeyer's discovery that pH imbalances could be detected by placing natural magnetic fields on the body. Dr. Goiz concluded that if imbalances could be detected, they could also be corrected. This realization led him to experiment with a new way of applying magnets to the body, and the results astonished him. He stated that he was able to help cure one of his HIV/AIDS patients, leading to the birth of a new scientific therapeutic field.

When I had the privilege of studying with Dr. Goiz in 2008, he challenged me to prove everything he said. I took his challenge seriously, and I have witnessed how this method has saved lives and improved the quality of life for individuals living with chronic pain. Just as Dr. Goiz told me, I'm telling you now: *don't believe everything I say, but go out and prove it for yourself.*

If the information you're about to read seems unbelievable or confusing, don't worry about it. All you need is a desire to take proactive steps towards living the best possible version of your life and an openness to try this therapy. I have seen countless cases where individuals, when ready to transform their lives, have achieved remarkable results. MPB is a scientific secret that is powerful, practical, precise, safe, effective, non-invasive, non-surgical, and non-chemical. It's a therapy that even children love.

By applying natural magnets to the body, MPB therapy has a direct effect at the atomic and molecular levels, aiding in the restoration of proper energy levels and erasing pH distortions. When the body is pH-balanced, it aides in homeostasis leading to better well-being. To understand the type of transformation that is possible, let's explore a few of the cases I've experienced:

Case 1: Diabetes, inflammation, eyesight, and aggression

I worked with a man in his late 50s who had been struggling with complications from diabetes. His eyesight was severely impaired, but the most significant issue for him was constant bloating that made him uncomfortable and perpetually irritable. After his first biomagnetic session, he immediately felt a positive shift and continued weekly sessions for a month. On his last visit, despite being an hour late due to heavy rain, he arrived in a surprisingly good mood. His ophthalmologist noticed a 5% improvement in his eyesight, which was deemed unusual under the circumstances, stated his doctor. This case is not isolated; similar outcomes are common, and more people are taking advantage of this miracle or blessing, as many have called it.

Case 2: Warts on fingers and lip

Another remarkable example involves a 13-year-old girl who had large, *juicy* (their words) warts on all ten fingers and her lip. Her mother indicated she had previously had the warts burned off with liquid nitrogen, but they only grew back larger. Seeking an alternative, they came for MPB therapy. Within a week, the warts began to shrink. By the second week, they were even smaller. In just 30 days, all her warts had disappeared without burning the skin or relying on lotions, potions, or diets. It was a complete resolution achieved through MPB.

Cases 3, 4, and 5: Infertility, pregnancy, and birth defects

Many women struggle with infertility, miscarriages, or the fear of giving birth to a child with defects. MPB has offered hope and solutions in these cases. I have personally helped several women achieve pregnancy, even in situations where they hadn't had a menstrual period for years.

One woman, after a single MPB session, conceived and eventually gave birth to a healthy baby. In another instance, a pregnant woman who experienced bleeding and a high risk of miscarriage sought biomagnetic therapy. The bleeding stopped on the same day of the session, and when the baby was born, an ovarian cyst that had caused the bleeding had disappeared.

Furthermore, I worked with a woman whose baby's Down Syndrome test initially came back positive early in her pregnancy. With subsequent biomagnetic sessions as part of her prenatal care, the Down Syndrome diagnosis was overturned, and she delivered a healthy boy.

Biomagnetism's ability to restore and maintain balance within the body contributes to these extraordinary outcomes. By seeking MPB both before and during pregnancy, individuals can optimize their chances of a healthy outcome for both mother and child.

Case 6: Irregular Menstruation Post COVID Vaccination

A 17-year-old girl experienced the sudden cessation of her menstrual periods within a month of receiving COVID vaccination. Over the subsequent year, her menstruation became irregular and extremely painful. Concerned, her family sought our MPB services. After her initial MPB session, her menstrual cycles returned to regularity, providing significant relief. When she returned for a follow-up session five months later, she reported sustained improvement in her menstrual health, plus noticing greater concentration levels, which was important to her since the first session, highlighting the positive impact of MPB therapy on her condition.

Case 7: Osteoarthritis Post COVID Vaccination

A physically active man in his mid-20s experienced hip pain two weeks after receiving the COVID vaccine. Months of medical visits yielded no definitive diagnosis until hip degeneration was evident in imaging, confirming osteoarthritis. Following his first MPB session, he experienced significant pain reduction within a week, allowing him to play sports again. Within a month, his walking improved, and he appeared less "waddled." Hopes are that with time, his cells will regenerate completely, though only time will tell. This case highlights the potential benefits of MPB therapy in alleviating post-vaccination health issues.

Remember, these are just a few examples of the transformative power of Biomagnetism. The therapy's true potential can only be understood through personal experience. I encourage you to approach it with an open mind and the willingness to prove its efficacy for yourself. You may be astonished by the results.

In the next chapter, we'll explore the practical application of MPB therapy and how you can begin experiencing its benefits firsthand.

Chapter 8

Biochemical Imbalances and the Power of Biomagnetism

"If you lose sight of the smaller accomplishments, you end up with an imbalance in your life."

– ALEXANDER MCCALL SMITH

You might be thinking, *I don't have digestive problems, diabetes, or warts,* and that's perfectly fine because Biomagnetism goes beyond addressing specific signs, symptoms, or diagnoses. It helps by detecting and erasing biochemical imbalances in the body, even when there are no apparent symptoms, or you've been told that the condition is incurable.

Many individuals go about their daily lives without realizing anything is wrong until a routine medical examination reveals something requiring further testing. Relying on pain or the results of medical exams to gauge your health and overall well-being is a misguided approach.

This is precisely why Biomagnetism is such a powerful and effective approach for everyone's existence and well-being. It should be considered not only as primary complimentary care for those who suffer but also as a way of life – a lifestyle, a habit, a routine – because striving for constant balance should be our daily goal.

From a biomagnetic perspective, we aim to detect and erase pH distortions and maintain pH balance, which is of utmost importance since our body is fundamentally based on biochemistry. Let's not forget that we're primarily composed of water, and water is made up of molecules, which in turn are made up of atoms that carry energy. We are absolute energy.

If the water within us is distorted, it negatively impacts the different dimensions of our existence – our mind, body, and spirituality. Unfortunately, we have become accustomed to compartmentalizing our existence, treating body parts or functions as separate entities. We believe that eye problems require a specialist, stomach issues require another, and psychological conflicts require yet another. This approach is misguided because all of our cells are interconnected. If even a single cell in our body suffers, the rest will suffer as well. Therefore, it's crucial to view ourselves as a whole and understand that any pain or symptom is a result of imbalance.

Biomagnetism provides a pathway to achieve balance. Our organism is constantly seeking balance and healing every day and every moment. This is the gift of life, and we should nourish our bodies with the energetic balance they need.

Factors that Cause Imbalance, Pain, Illness, and Disease

To lead a fulfilling life and realize our dreams, we must be aware of the factors that distort our biochemistry and cause us suffering.

Living with awareness allows us to overcome ignorance and fear, fostering personal improvement and benefiting humanity as a whole.

The factors that lead to biochemical imbalances and subsequent disorder and diseases include:

1. *Pathogens/Infections:* Viruses, bacteria, parasites, and fungi.

2. *Dysfunctions:* Glandular, organ, or systemic dysfunctions (e.g., nervous, circulatory).

3. *Toxins:* Environmental toxins, food toxins, medication toxins, nutritional supplement toxins, pathogen toxins, and more.

4. *Psychological:* Psychiatric, emotional, and belief system factors.

5. *Emotional Trauma*: Unexpected shocks and traumatic experiences.

6. *Deficiencies:* Mineral deficiencies, vitamin deficiencies, and dehydration.

7. *Spiritual Health:* A lack of a sense of purpose and connection to one's spirituality.

8. *Foreign DNA:* Blood transfusions, organ transplants, vaccines and other factors introducing foreign DNA into the body.

9. *Malignancy:* Negative emotions directed at you by others, such as anger, hatred, and jealousy.

10. *Chakra Imbalances*: Blocked energy vortexes within the body.

All these factors mentioned above distort your biochemistry and affect your health in various ways. They can cause fatigue, impair decision-making abilities, dampen your sense of purpose, induce pain, and even lead to death.

Biomagnetism aims to erase these biochemical imbalances – the root causes – and that is why most conditions improve after just one to two sessions. By creating internal biochemical balance through the application of magnetic fields, we can erase pH distortions. This incredible method, coupled with wellness-supporting lifestyle habits, is undoubtedly an optimal approach to healing the mind, body, and spirit. It's safe, natural, and honors the standard of quality of life you deserve.

Infections and the Allopathic Medical System

It's commonly believed that when you're sick, you need medication, such as antibiotics, to get better. However, millions of people worldwide, either by conscious choice or lack of access, do not take medication and yet are not dead or suffering indefinitely. With extensive marketing by pharmaceutical companies and coercion at the highest levels of government in the name of public health, many people fail to recognize that the body has the perfect ability to heal itself as long as we give it what it needs, for example, nutrient-rich nourishment, exercise, positive thinking, Biomagnetism for biochemical balancing and other natural resources that support body function. We must also avoid harmful behaviors that would cancel out these well-being actions, such as substance abuse, junk "food" that affects our microbiome, and other.

Often, people are quick to rush to a medical doctor at the first sign of physical pain, believing that a test and a pill will fix their problem. In many cases, the reality is quite the opposite. Test results may indicate an infection, but the prescribed antibiotic may cause more problems, leading to the prescription of stronger medications for drug resistant infections, while the problem worsens, or adverse reaction due to poisoning and debilitated physiological mechanisms. Be aware that medication is not intended to strengthen body function; it's mostly a means to numb pain, kill infections, which of course are also killing our healthy cells and microbiome, and forcefully regulating functions, for example, sugar levels.

Relying solely on medication is a failed system. The World Health Organization has acknowledged that medicines are failing against many infections due to microbial evolution and increasing resistance to the pharmaceutical approach. Yet, most people continue to rely on medical doctors because they believe it's the only scientifically proven source of help. But are you truly certain about that?

As one medical doctor told me, "Diagnosing a patient is more an art than a science." If the medical system were purely science-based, why do medical errors, misdiagnoses, and mistreatments occur daily? Moreover, why do developed countries with ample access to medical care experience increasing rates of disease? Why are more people getting sick and why are more hospitals being constructed?

My point is that the allopathic medical system leaves many unanswered questions. Rather than detecting and addressing the underlying causes of disease, patients often manage their pain through medications and surgeries. And what about the medical tests you undergo? In most cases, they merely photograph or describe symptoms once there is a visible manifestation.

There are numerous questions that science cannot answer at this time. For instance, why does a bacterium like E. Coli, which is naturally present in the intestines, turn hostile and attack us? While we may not have the answers to such questions, Dr. Goiz's biomagnetic discovery suggests that the key lies not in understanding why this happens but in having the ability to solve this infectious problem using safe and cost-effective magnetic fields.

Infections and Biomagnetism

Dr. Goiz realized that infections create simultaneous pH distortions in the body. For example, if E. Coli is an active infection, it will cause specific pH imbalances (acidity *and* alkalinity) in the *thymus* gland and the *liver*.

With MPB, we do not rely on blood tests or any other type of machinery-based testing to determine what is wrong in the body. Instead, by applying magnetic fields to specific areas of the body, we observe a reflex response, often manifesting as a leg length discrepancy. This reflex tells us, a pH distortion has been identified, and we simultaneously apply positive and negative field magnets to correct these issues.

Many of you may have already visited doctors who failed to determine what is wrong with you, with inconclusive blood work and other tests. You may have been told, *"Nothing is wrong with you."* But why do you still feel miserable?

This is precisely why in the biomagnetic field we do not fully depend on conventional medical testing, as test results often fail to provide a reliable picture. Through Biomagnetism, the strategic placement of both negative (north) and positive (south) poles to specific anatomical areas, we not only identify where biochemical imbalances occur but also apply the solution using the same magnets to erase those imbalances.

By erasing pH imbalances, pathogens cannot continue reproducing or attacking the organism because we have eliminated the pH-distorted environments that infections require to thrive. When the body achieves pH balance, infections cannot persist, and the body can heal and repair itself. Through the simple and safe application of magnets to the body, many people are finding healing and well-being in situations where natural solutions, such as for cancer and other chronic degenerative diseases, seemed elusive.

Chapter 9

The Limitations of Medicines: Exploring Alternative Paths to Healing

"Half of the modern drugs could well be thrown out of the window, except that the birds might eat them."

– DR. MARTIN HENRY FISCHER

The limitations of medicine become evident when it comes to addressing issues that stem from underlying spiritual-emotional challenges. Using pharmaceutical solutions to numb the pain or discomfort caused by emotional stress is futile because it fails to address the root of the problem. Instead, it's more meaningful to dive deep within oneself, identify proactive steps for overcoming emotional hurt, and take responsibility for one's own feelings. By doing so, we can avoid creating more problems by ignoring our emotional pain and denying ourselves the opportunity for healing.

Biomagnetism offers a valuable approach to dealing with emotional factors because emotions have a direct impact on our biochemistry. Emotional stress can lead to specific pH imbalances in organs and glands. Through the application of magnets, Biomagnetism helps restore balance to the body and enables individuals to more easily free themselves from feelings of *sadness*, *anger*, and other confusing and painful emotions. It's crucial for individuals to actively work towards avoiding falling into the same emotional traps and to identify the underlying emotional blockages. Biomagnetism not only promotes relaxation but also targets the source of the problem by erasing the pH distortions caused by emotions.

While Biomagnetism is often not associated with emotional issues, an increasing number of people are discovering its effectiveness. For example, consider the case of a man who sought my help after a painful romantic breakup. He experienced difficulty concentrating at work, sleep problems, and unhealthy weight loss. After a biomagnetic session, he reported feeling different, experiencing strong vibrations in his head, seeing vivid lights, and feeling more relaxed. The next day, he slept well and felt better equipped to cope with his broken heart. This is just one example of how Biomagnetism can bring about positive transformation in emotional well-being.

Emotions have the power to create specific pH distortions in the body, and Biomagnetism works by restoring energetic balance. Let's take the example of *rage*, a common emotion. Instead of relying solely on endless hours of psychotherapy to deal with rage, Biomagnetism focuses on identifying and addressing the root emotion. By applying magnets to specific areas associated with the emotion, such as the *liver* and *heart*, balance can be restored.

Healing is a process, and Biomagnetism serves as a powerful, practical, and effective tool to support that process. It's essential to recognize that emotional well-being plays a significant role in overall health, especially in chronic or degenerative diseases. Unresolved emotions can distort biochemistry, creating an internal environment conducive to the development of infections and dysfunctions. By addressing emotional well-being and belief systems, individuals can take important steps towards healing. Transforming negativity into positivity and practicing self-forgiveness are key aspects of this process.

It's worth acknowledging the opposition faced by Biomagnetism and its discoverer, Dr. Goiz Durán, M.D. The potential of Biomagnetism to disrupt the multibillion-dollar pharmaceutical and medical industry has resulted in resistance from powerful entities. Organizations that depend on diseases for their survival may resist the dissemination of this, and other helpful life-enhancing information. Dr. Goiz's breakthrough discovery has been met with rejection from influential organizations, not due to its lack of truth but because it threatens the profits of the rich and powerful. The healthcare system and its cohort's motivations and its prioritization of political and economic factors over individual well-being are now absolutely apparent in this post COVID era.

As more people awaken to these realities, they are discovering that the very healthcare system they turn to for help can be a significant contributor to illness, suffering and premature death. For too long, these forces have deceived us into believing that nature is ineffective and that only laboratories hold the answers to our health. This perpetuates a cycle of pain and suffering rather than addressing the root causes.

In most cases, Biomagnetism can provide substantial help. While belief in the process is important, it's the individual's action and responsibility for their own well-being that truly makes a difference. Healing is a personal journey, and being open to seeking help and taking inspired action are crucial steps. Biomagnetism can yield remarkable results for individuals and their families, as diseases impact everyone. Even in end-stage situations, Biomagnetism can contribute to improving the quality of life.

Safety is a priority in Biomagnetism, and practitioners aim to ensure a positive experience. In general, applying magnets is safe, even for individuals who are pregnant, have surgical implants, taking medications, or undergoing other therapies. However, it's important to note that Biomagnetism initiates a healing process that can affect medication dosages. Meaning, if, for example, your blood sugar levels improve, then the existing dosage for sugar-controlling pills must be modified. Close attention should be paid to changes in the body's response to medication, and consultation with the prescribing medical doctor may be necessary to adjust dosages accordingly. For individuals with metallic implants, Biomagnetism poses no harm as medical implants are non-magnetic.

In summary, Biomagnetism is a safe, natural and effective approach that can offer transformative results. Temporary healing crises that cause increased annoyance, such as frequent restroom visits or fatigue, may occur but are a positive sign of the body detoxifying and going through transformation. By embracing Biomagnetism and taking an active role in one's well-being, individuals can experience profound improvements in their health and quality of life.

Chapter 10

Distinguishing Magnet Therapy, Medical Biomagnetism, and Recalibration Biomagnetism

"Seek first to understand, then to be understood."

- STEPHEN R. COVEY

Magnet Therapy (MT) and Medical Pair Biomagnetism (MPB) represent two distinct approaches to utilizing magnetic fields for healing purposes. While MT involves the application of magnetic fields to specific sites of pain or discomfort, MPB takes a more comprehensive approach by detecting and correcting specific pH imbalances caused by various factors, including microorganisms, toxins, and emotional factors.

In MT, individuals may use magnetic products such as necklaces, rings, bracelets, or even mattresses, or they may place magnets directly on or near the affected area of concern. The therapy typically relies on knowing which side of the magnet carries the negative field, as that is the field typically used towards the body in this methodology. It's important to note that MT is not a diagnostic method and does not targets specific pH distortions or address mental and spiritual issues.

In contrast, MPB offers a powerful, precise, and effective approach to healing. It focuses on restoring the body's biochemistry balance by identifying and correcting specific pH distortions caused by underlying factors that contribute to illness. This therapeutic approach is rooted in a theoretical scientific medical foundation and is capable of diagnosing and treating diseases from a pH perspective.

Trained practitioners of MPB undergo specialized training to apply magnetic pairs (combinations of negative and positive fields) with a focused mind, body, and spirit medical purpose. They utilize this therapy to address not only physical ailments but also mind-spirit imbalances, providing a holistic approach to healing.

Recalibration Biomagnetism (RB) builds upon the foundation of MPB but incorporates elements of quantum physics and energy medicine. RB places a strong emphasis on energetic recalibration, seeking to rebalance the body's energy fields and optimize its overall functioning. In RB, magnets are placed strategically on points associated with energy flow in the body, aiming to recalibrate and optimize energetic patterns. This approach facilitates self-healing, restoring balance on physical, mental, emotional, and spiritual levels. It underscores the role of intention and consciousness in the healing process.

The RB method was developed to make the principles of biomagnetic pairing more accessible to individuals. It provides a user-friendly guide to utilizing biomagnetic therapy for self-care, incorporating wellness protocols that promote mind-body-spirit balance, pain management, detoxification, and overall optimization of body systems for holistic wellness.

Biomagnetism offers an exciting alternative to expensive, invasive, and often unsatisfactory hospital visits. As more people recognize the limitations of mainstream allopathic medicine, they are turning to both MPB and RB for their potential to address various health conditions that were previously considered incurable, as well as for prevention.

Due to the limited availability of qualified biomagnetic specialists worldwide, finding a practitioner can be challenging. This is where the RB method can play a crucial role in one's self-care strategies. Understanding the differences between MT, MPB, and RB, empowers individuals to make informed decisions about their health and explore alternative avenues for healing and well-being.

Chapter 11

Convenient Professional Help: Distance Healing and the BiomagScan Services

"Distance is just a test to see how far love can travel."

– UNKNOWN

The belief that access to Medical Pair Biomagnetism (MPB) is limited due to the scarcity of therapists worldwide is wrong. In reality, Biomagnetism is accessible to everyone on earth, regardless of their location, even in remote areas. Every day, we're helping individuals from faraway places reclaim control over their lives and restoring balance, leading to optimal quality of life. This remarkable feat is achieved through the *Biomagnetic Distance Healing* methodology.

Initially, Distance Healing may seem unfamiliar or unconventional. I, too, had reservations about it initially. However, after years of practice and observation, I can confidently attest to its efficacy, comparable to in-person treatments at our center.

Recently, I had the opportunity to perform Distance Healing for two women who had been hospitalized for an extended period. One was afflicted with Guillain-Barre Syndrome, leading to paralysis, while the other battled lung cancer. Astonishingly, both individuals experienced immediate improvements. The woman with Guillain-Barre Syndrome was discharged that week and transferred to a rehabilitation facility, while the woman with lung cancer gained more energy and experienced enhanced breathing.

The methodology we employ in Biomagnetic Distance Healing involves placing magnets on a person who is not the intended recipient. In the aforementioned cases, the brother of one woman and the daughter of the other acted as surrogates. If a relative were unable to participate, one of our in-house assistants would have assumed the role of a surrogate to transmit the therapeutic effect over the distance. It's crucial to note that Distance Healing is only conducted with the explicit consent of the intended recipient. For children, consent is unnecessary as it's the parent's responsibility to make decisions on their behalf.

Through this scientific approach, we demonstrate that we can initiate a biochemical shift in a person, regardless of their physical distance from us.

The concept of Distance Healing may challenge conventional scientific paradigms, as it raises questions about how a therapist can influence the cells of an individual located on the opposite side of the world. However, the truth lies in the understanding that our DNA holds the answers to many of our ailments, and we have the ability to communicate healing to our DNA.

Researchers such as Dr. Esther del Rio and Dr. Masaru Emoto, who explore the properties of water, have shown that our intentions can produce structural and informational changes in water crystals within our bodies and external to us. Considering that our bodies consist mostly of water, this understanding opens avenues for deeper exploration of psychological, emotional, and spiritual obstacles. Ongoing scientific research contributes to our understanding of how Distance Healing becomes possible.

By comprehending the true nature of our obstacles, we gain the ability to shift our thoughts and actions, overcoming multidimensional barriers and reclaiming control over our lives. This empowerment allows us to reach the destination we genuinely desire – a state of being in control.

The accessibility of MPB has long been a concern for those seeking effective treatment. With only a handful of practitioners worldwide, this therapy has remained largely unknown and misunderstood by the majority of the world's population. Moreover, traditional in-person sessions with certified practitioners have made it difficult for those in remote areas or with limited mobility to access this treatment, and for some the distance healing method provokes skepticism. But, thanks to our personalized biomagnetic illustration services (*BiomagScan*), MPB is now accessible to anyone, anywhere; needing only a phone or internet connection to communicate and magnets for self-application.

The BiomagScan service is a cutting-edge health service that combines the power of MPB with the convenience of modern technology. Our growing team of expert biomagnetic practitioners has developed a unique program to provide you with the guidance and support you need to achieve optimal health and wellness.

How does the MagnoGuide work?

To get started, simply purchase the BiomagScan service through *www.SaveMeMagnets.com*, and you'll receive an email with instructions on how to send in basic information about yourself (or recipient), including *your name, date of birth, geographic location, symptoms,* and any other relevant health history details.

Next, M. Durazo, or another certified biomagnetic specialist, will review your information and create a personalized treatment plan specifically for you. This plan will include a diagram indicating where to place the magnets on your body for optimal results. By doing so you're receiving the direct benefits of MPB from the convenience of wherever you're located.

Please note that for this BiomagScan service, you'll need a set of magnets. It's essential to use the SaveMeMagnets.com brand to ensure that you have correctly labeled magnets.

Once you receive your personalized illustration, you can begin your treatment right away. It's incredibly easy to use, and you don't need any prior knowledge or experience with MPB to benefit from it. All you need to do is follow the instructions and place the magnets on your body as directed, right in the comfort of your own home.

Why should you start using the BiomagScan?

The BiomagScan offers numerous benefits for those seeking to improve their health and well-being:

- *Convenience:* Access your health program from anywhere, at any time.

- *Personalized* attention: Connect with your biomagnetic practitioner for individualized support and guidance.

- *Affordability:* The program is available at a fraction of the cost of in-person biomagnetic therapy, with no travel or time off from work required.

- *Easy to use:* The program is designed to be user-friendly and accessible to individuals of all ages and backgrounds.

- *Effectiveness:* Biomagnetism has been shown to be a powerful tool for improving health and well-being, with countless success stories from individuals who have used this therapy.

Don't let chronic pain and illness hold you back from living your best life. Start using BiomagScan today and experience the power of MPB for yourself.

Can I treat my pet with Biomagnetism?

Yes, it's possible to treat your pets with MPB. The most convenient way to do this is to treat pets via Biomagnetic Distance Healing. Again, this method involves placing magnets on a surrogate, directing consciousness and intention to address the pet's health.

In the next chapter, we'll explore another powerful approach within the topic of energy balancing and hands-on healing – the Alphabiotic spinal alignments – and uncover the potential for optimizing our mind-body-spirit connection.

Chapter 12

Alphabiotics: Awakening Inner Peace and Balance Through Touch

*"To keep the body in good health is a duty... otherwise we
shall not be able to keep our mind strong and clear."*

- BUDDHA

O ne day, a television personality visited our healing center for
an interview, and I had the opportunity to provide him with
an Alphabiotic spinal alignment. The following day, I was amazed
at the visible transformation in his appearance. With a wide smile,
he eagerly shook my hand and shared his experience. He had been
facing work-related stress and problems throughout the week
but immediately after the spinal alignment, he felt a profound
sense of peace and happiness. Not only that, but the solution to
his work-related issue came to him like a lightning bolt soon after
leaving our center.

Around the same time, a woman came to me seeking relief from severe neck pain. She worked as a hotel room cleaner, and a week prior, a colleague accidentally dropped towels from the second floor, landing on her head. Contemplating a visit to the doctor, she decided to give the Alphabiotic alignment a try. To her surprise, the pain vanished immediately after the alignment.

To understand Alphabiotics, we must acknowledge that every aspect of our existence is composed of energy. From this fundamental premise, we can explore life and its various dimensions. Energy permeates everything around us, encompassing emotions such as love, happiness, sadness, rage, pain, good health, and poor health. These different vibrations of energy within us determine the difference between optimal high energy levels that promote well-being and low energetic levels that lead to ill health.

When touch is applied to our bodies with the focused intention to heal or transform, it has the power to turn anxiety, anger, and frustration into peace and well-being. The power of touch is undeniable, and its effects can be observed even without specific training or methods. A heartfelt hug between loved ones, for example, can immediately shift the energy within both individuals. Touch has the ability to move energy.

However, touch goes beyond mere mechanics. The intention and state of mind behind the touch play a crucial role. A mechanical or angry touch will evoke different feelings compared to a touch filled with love and compassion. This highlights the significance of touch as a powerful healing modality.

There are numerous hands-on therapeutic techniques that contribute to our overall well-being. My journey with therapeutic touch began with an Acupressure class I attended at the university, which proved to be an eye-opening and transformative experience. Over the years, I have explored various types of hands-on healing work, including Massage (utilizing many techniques), Reflexology, Reiki, Chiropractic, and Alphabiotics – the focus of this chapter.

It's important to recognize the inherent value in each of these touch therapies, especially when both the practitioner and recipient work together towards a common goal. As a recipient, your objective should be to achieve and maintain physical, emotional, and spiritual balance.

The essence of Alphabiotics lies in helping us become more conscious, spiritual, alert, and fully alive. It goes beyond merely addressing physical ailments resulting from a misaligned spine or attempting to manipulate specific vertebrae into a predetermined position. Alphabiotics involves understanding the underlying issues that cause muscle tension and misalignment in the spine. By engaging in Alphabiotic alignments, the vertebrae naturally fall into their appropriate places, awakened by our innate energy's desire for peace and balance.

Everyday stressors contribute to imbalance, and it's crucial to return our bodies to a unified state of balance. When we achieve internal unity, guidance emerges from within, leading to strength in all aspects of life. We gain a deeper understanding of ourselves, foster better relationships, enhance creativity, intuition, experience joy, and more.

Conversely, when we experience inner separation, imbalance, or allow external influences to overpower us, our vital energy disperses outward, resulting in weakness, inefficiency, and pain. Unbalanced individuals often adopt a victim mentality, attributing their problems to external factors rather than acknowledging the role their attitude plays in perpetuating a low-energy existence.

Alphabiotics, combined with Medical and Recalibration Biomagnetism, is an opportunity to reclaim our power and shift our thinking and actions to overcome multidimensional barriers, enabling us to regain control of our lives. It's not about fixing something that is wrong but rather tapping into the immense potential within each of us. Alphabiotics aligns us with the essence of what is right – our innate capacity for perfect well-being and the infinite possibilities for living a fulfilling life.

Within each of us resides an intelligent life force that empowers us to solve problems, manifest dreams, experience peace, harmony, and maintain a constant state of physical, emotional, and spiritual balance. Regular Alphabiotic alignments provide a solid solution to live consciously, set intentions, grow, prosper, find peace, and more.

It's crucial to move away from the notion that we must be in obvious pain or emotional suffering to seek wellness solutions. Instead, we must embrace Biomagnetism and Alphabiotics as integral parts of our lifestyle, just like brushing our teeth or showering. Recognizing the need for an alignment to address my own physical and mental fatigue, I understand the immediate benefits of Alphabiotics and the urgency to take action.

Recognizing the signs of balance issues is essential, as a person's posture can reveal whether they are unified or unbalanced. Contracted, tight, or weak muscles indicate an imbalance. Look at yourself in the mirror – do you notice one shoulder or hip higher than the other? Are you slouching? Is your head tilted to one side? Lack of bilateral symmetry suggests muscular weakness, tension, and obstructed energy flow.

Self-consciousness and self-awareness play vital roles in living a better life. By going beyond the notion that something is wrong and instead focusing on our ability to live with optimal energetic levels at all times, we gain the power to take control of our well-being.

Most of us have a dominant brain hemisphere, resulting in one side of the body being stronger than the other. Stress, which is a constant in our lives, exacerbates this asymmetry. As the dominant brain hemisphere causes corresponding muscles to contract, one side of the body tightens while the other weakens. This imbalance can lead to leg length discrepancies and other issues.

Alphabiotics aims to unify brain hemispheres, bringing balance to the body's strength and function and disrupting stress patterns. By engaging in Alphabiotic alignments, we can restore balance and live in a state of optimal energy levels consistently.

The spine encases the nervous system, which is responsible for the body's proper functioning. Any interference in the nervous system can lead to a range of problems. Stress-induced muscle tightening bends the spine, exerting pressure on the nerves and hindering the flow of energy. Alphabiotic alignments involve hands-on impulses applied to the spine, liberating the body from physical, emotional, and spiritual stress. The result is immediate inner peace, balance, and improved overall function.

While Alphabiotics may share similarities with Chiropractic, including the production of a popping sound in the spine, they are distinct modalities. Chiropractic focuses on medical diagnoses and correcting specific vertebrae through spinal adjustments, aiming to remove blockages and facilitate healing. In contrast, Alphabiotics prioritizes lifestyle and supports optimal living. Alphabiotic alignments engage the entire spine lengthwise, allowing for a comprehensive approach to balance and well-being.

When performed by a properly trained Alphabioticist, the alignments are safe and effective. A skilled practitioner ensures the safety of individuals of all ages, including infants, facilitating inner peace and balance. Pregnant women and those planning to conceive can also benefit from Alphabiotics, as it helps alleviate the physical and emotional stresses associated with pregnancy. While Alphabiotics is generally safe, individuals who have recently undergone spinal surgery should wait until they have fully healed before considering alignments.

The frequency of Alphabiotic alignments, like any wellness modality, varies based on individual factors such as finances, time availability, and personal desire. A minimum of six alignments per year is a good starting point. Personally, I would receive Alphabiotics daily if I had easy access to it. Living consciously empowers us to determine the optimal frequency of alignments for ensuring our well-being.

It's disheartening that many people neglect to take action when it comes to their health. We readily maintain and repair our vehicles, electronics, and appliances, but often disregard our own well-being until we can no longer function properly. This approach can have dire consequences, including loss of life. It's vital to recalibrate ourselves regularly through practices like Biomagnetism and Alphabiotics to maintain optimal health.

Fear often prevents individuals from seeking help. Medical visits and invasive procedures can be intimidating and disempowering. However, Alphabiotics does not focus on finding what's wrong within us but rather on unlocking our innate potential for well-being.

It's about helping individuals live better while embracing the fact that everything is right with them.

In writing this book, my goal is to save you years of study, thousands of dollars, and the frustration of chasing ineffective cures. I want to empower you to prioritize your well-being and take action to live a fulfilling and balanced life. Embrace the fact that you're capable of achieving optimal energetic levels and embark on a journey of self-discovery and self-care.

Chapter 13

Internal Rejuvenating Exercises for Optimal Health

"Focus enough energy inward. Before befriending others, you have to be your own friends. Before making others happy, you have to make yourself happy. It's not called selfishness; it's called personal development."

– MELCHER LIM

A few months ago, I had the opportunity to work with an individual who had started an exercise routine to cope with the extreme stress of going through a divorce, managing a full-time job, and pursuing a higher education degree. While, according to him, he was in the best physical shape of his life, he constantly felt tired and struggled to focus. It became apparent that although he made the right choice to exercise, the demanding nature and excessive duration of his routine were having an adverse effect on his physical and emotional well-being. This chapter explores the importance of exercise moderation and introduces internal rejuvenating exercises that can help us maintain optimal health without causing harm.

Recognizing Energy Depletion from Exercise

It's imperative to recognize that exercise is not a one-size-fits-all solution. What may be beneficial and energizing for one person could pose serious risks or harm to another. Each individual has unique physical capabilities and limitations, and it's crucial to listen to our bodies and adapt our exercise routines accordingly. In the case mentioned, we employed the bioenergetic technique of muscle testing to determine the optimal exercise regimen for the individual. Through this process, it was revealed that the individual needed to reduce their exercise intensity or duration. As a result, the individual experienced significant improvements in their well-being, highlighting the importance of understanding our personal limits to avoid depleting our energy reserves.

By the way, if you're interested in learning the bioenergetic muscle-testing technique, you can acquire the Recalibration System kit and/ or on-demand course. The physical kit is available on the Amazon platform. Alternatively, if you require international shipping, please visit *www.SaveMeMagnets.com* to contact us for further assistance in obtaining the kit. Also, you may gain access to the on-demand course at the same website.

The Power of Internal Rejuvenating Exercises

While there are numerous types of exercises available, our ancestors discovered centuries ago that internal exercises hold immense power and are suitable for everyone. By focusing on our thinking, breathing, and movement, these exercises revitalize our physiological and mental functions, making external exercises unnecessary. Internal exercises strengthen our internal organ systems, such as the heart, liver, kidneys, and digestive system, in unique ways that external exercises cannot replicate. They help us feel younger, fresher, and more energetic, promoting overall well-being.

Understanding the Three Internal Rejuvenating Exercises

Throughout history, our ancestors observed that certain animals, such as the crane, the turtle, and the deer, lived remarkably long lives. They adopted the movements of these animals as exercises for human use. Here, we introduce three basic yet powerful internal rejuvenating exercises that can provide immense benefits.

1. *The Crane Exercise:* When our digestive, respiratory, and circulatory systems face issues, we may experience various symptoms, such as constipation, diarrhea, bloating, indigestion, and poor circulation. The ancients discovered that crane birds stimulate and strengthen their corresponding systems by folding a leg into their belly. We adapted this action for human use in the Crane Exercise. This exercise can be done in different positions – standing, sitting, or lying on your back – and involves placing your hands on either side of your belly button. Slowly inhale through the nose, and as you exhale, gently push down with your palms, imagining harmful microorganisms and emotional obstacles leaving your lungs. Aim to complete 12 rounds of this exercise, focusing on slow and deliberate breathing. The Crane Exercise induces a calming effect, allowing relaxation and nourishment of the body as energy flows to areas that need assistance.

2. *The Deer Exercise:* The strength of our anal sphincter muscle serves as an indicator of our overall health and is closely linked to our sexual gland's energy in both males and females. Weak sexual glands correspond to a weak anal sphincter, while strong sexual glands indicate a strong anal

sphincter. By observing deer, the ancients noticed that they exercise their anus by contracting it while wiggling their tails. This led to the development of the Deer Exercise. By contracting the anal muscles upward and inward as hard as possible and holding the contraction, we stimulate the prostate gland (in males) and promote the secretion of euphoriant hormones that regulate the endocrine system. This exercise offers numerous benefits, including the strengthening of the anal sphincter, improved sexual function, hormone balance, and prevention of sexual disorders. The Deer Exercise can be performed in various positions and is recommended in the morning, before bed, and even before engaging in sexual activity.

3. *The Turtle Exercise:* The neck area acts as a bridge between our brain and the nerves that control our entire body. Keeping this bridge free of tension and blockages is vital. The Turtle Exercise is a self-help exercise that stretches the entire spine, strengthens shoulder muscles, and relieves tiredness, stiffness, and soreness in the neck and shoulders. Additionally, it stimulates and strengthens the thyroid and parathyroid glands, thereby improving metabolism and promoting overall energy. To perform the Turtle Exercise, start by bringing your chin down towards your chest while extending your head outwards like a turtle. Inhale deeply during this step. Next, bring the back of your head down as if touching the back of your neck, while shrugging your shoulders upwards. Exhale during this motion. Repeat this exercise at least 12 times, focusing on slow and deliberate breathing.

Embracing Internal Rejuvenating Exercises

As you incorporate these internal rejuvenating exercises into your routine, it's important to note that you may initially experience sensations or discomfort that are new to you. However, rest assured that these exercises are safe, effective, and easy to perform. Pain or discomfort may indicate the flow of energy being restored in neglected areas. Over time, you can combine these exercises and customize them to your preference. By practicing these exercises, you empower yourself to overcome disease, maintain higher energy levels, and age fearlessly. Remember, these exercises are meant to enhance your overall well-being and should be performed with patience, consistency, and self-awareness.

Chapter 14

The Power of Nutrition

"Take care of your body. It's the only place you have to live."
– JIM ROHN

L ife is about more than any particular therapy, technique, or intervention – fundamentally, it's tied to our lifestyle. The manner in which we fuel our bodies significantly affects our mind, body, and spirit equilibrium. Do the food choices we make nourish the life we aspire to, or do they lead to fatigue and potential sickness?

Indeed, the food we consume is integral to clear thinking, a healthy body, and even our spiritual interpretation of life's purpose. It's undeniably true that we are, in every respect, what we eat. While proponents of dietary supplements might urge the need for multivitamins and minerals, it's essential to remember that these nutrients are readily available in natural foods. If we consciously maintain a healthy diet, we're likely ingesting enough of these vital elements.

The task of deciding the correct amounts of calcium, and vitamins X, Y, and Z we require, without disturbing our inner harmony and inadvertently causing ourselves harm, is a legitimate concern. While supplements might be necessary in certain cases due to malnourishment leading to nutritional deficiencies, it's vital to comprehend the significant difference in the quality of available supplements.

The truth is, no supplement can genuinely duplicate the benefits provided by nature through a balanced diet. By choosing to eat natural foods, we can obtain all the minerals and vitamins necessary for achieving and maintaining optimal health.

Yet, it's important to realize that if our body's pH is imbalanced, nutrient assimilation might be hindered, regardless of our dietary choices or supplement consumption. Therefore, restoring our appropriate pH balance through Biomagnetism is essential for peak function.

In the previous version of this book, I referenced the Taoist philosophy that promotes pH-balanced eating, and the Paleo diet that is modeled after our Paleolithic ancestors' eating habits. Although I still believe there is value in both understandings, I believe we can simplify this conversation further, rather than getting into the specific topic of cutting out high-sugar and starchy foods, because the truth is that not all sugars are created or consumed equally.

I recently discovered video-lectures given by Dr. Robert Lustig, M.D. who talks about the grave dangers of sugar consumption. At the end of one of the talks that both my 9 year old son and I listened to, Dr. Lustig simplified a way to determine what foods to eat. He described there being four categories of foods ranging by how much human processing occurred with those foods.

The example he gave for category one was an unprocessed apple picked from the tree. The example given for category two foods is a sliced apple – there is now human interaction. The example for category three foods is to take that apple and convert it into apple sauce, but not adding anything to it. And finally, the example for category four foods are baking an apple cake where now you have several ingredients and is now void of fiber, diminished nutritional value, and causing intoxication and destruction of the guts' microbiome from the sugars and preservatives. His research has lead to the conclusion that ONLY category four foods are directly connected to illness.

There's a high chance that once you adapt this natural-foods way of eating (categories 1-4), you won't want to revert back to processed foods because the energy you gain will be unmatchable. Shopping mainly in the produce and lean protein sections will get you on track with this diet. Include healthy fats like coconut oil, raw olive oil, or ghee (clarified butter), and you're on your way to success. This diet mirrors the eating habits of many cultures in the East today, which are rich in locally grown vegetables and supplemented with small amounts of protein.

The question of which fats or oils to cook with is crucial. My parents grew up consuming lard as a dietary staple, but my siblings and I were raised on vegetable and seed oils. Why the change? Well, at a certain point in our nutritional education, we were warned against animal fats, leading restaurants and food manufacturers to switch to vegetable and seed oils. However, studies indicate that cooking with vegetable and seed oils can be incredibly harmful, while cooking with animal fats is not as detrimental as we were led to believe.

This reminds me of a humorous analogy of how medical advice has evolved over time:

- **2000 BC:** Eat this root.

- **1000 AD:** That root is heathen. Say this prayer.

- **1800 AD:** That prayer is superstitious. Drink this potion.

- **1900 AD:** That potion is snake oil. Swallow this pill.

- **1950 AD:** That pill is ineffective. Take this antibiotic.

- **2024 AD:** That antibiotic is artificial, ineffective, harmful, and heathen. Eat this root, pray, meditate. Seek Biomagnetism for your medicine, roots for your nutrition, prayer for spirituality, and Alphabiotics for stress management.

Over time, certain foods have gone through a cycle of being labeled as good and healthy, then bad and unhealthy, and then reverting back to being highly nutritious. This is the current debate surrounding animal fats, with many now advocating that animal fats are the best for cooking, while vegetable and seed oils are highly toxic.

To comprehend why we need to stop cooking with vegetable and seed oils immediately, we need to understand the following: Vegetable and seed oils are prone to oxidation. If you're unsure of what oxidation is, you've likely witnessed it before. For instance, what happens when you bite into an apple or slice an avocado and leave it exposed to oxygen? They change color, with the apple browning and the avocado darkening. This is oxidation. You've seen the same process occur when metals rust, or oxidize, after exposure to water and oxygen.

This oxidation in food results in a harmful chemical alteration. Vegetable and seed oils, particularly when heated, oxidize easily, leading to rancidity. This process also occurs when raw materials, like corn, olives, and seeds, are pressed to extract their oils, which involves exposure to heat. If these ingredients are then added to a frying pan, the situation worsens.

High-quality oils that haven't been excessively pressed, like olive oil that has been pressed just once, can have delightful raw flavors. However, rancid olive oil will have a noticeably different smell and taste. The issue with relying on taste and smell to judge the quality of healthy vegetable oils like olive or avocado is that modern extraction techniques using chemical solvents often employ deodorizers to mask any odors. This simply adds another layer of toxicity!

When the fatty acids break down during oxidation, they lose their nutritional value and produce free radicals. Free radicals are atoms with an odd number of electrons, which can cause cellular damage, speeding up aging and contributing to inflammation. In simple terms, consuming oxidized substances leads to the degeneration of our bodies, making us more susceptible to pain, suffering, and disease.

That's where antioxidants come into play, as these molecules can safely interact with free radicals, countering the harmful effects of oxidation. Antioxidants include micronutrients like vitamin E, beta-carotene, and vitamin C. It's important to note that these micronutrients are naturally present in our foods – a point we'll dive into further in the next chapter. Mother Nature is the best pharmacist, and her remedies are readily available in the produce section of your local grocery store.

Another significant issue with vegetable and seed oils is their high Omega-6 content. Omega-6 and Omega-3 are both essential polyunsaturated fats necessary for human health, but a balance must be maintained for proper function. Our ancestors likely consumed roughly equal amounts of both Omegas, but modern diets often tip the scale with excessive Omega-6 intake. This overconsumption gradually leads to cellular inflammation, compromising our entire body's function, weakening digestion and immune responses, and making us more vulnerable to microbes.

Poor nutrition can also impact the nervous system, affecting physical mobility and thought processes, leading to negative feelings and self-destructive actions. It's crucial to remember that everything we consume affects us. Many of the oils used in processed foods, restaurants, and even our homes include easily oxidized polyunsaturated fats and pro-inflammatory Omega-6 fatty acids.

The goal here is harm reduction. It's almost impossible to completely avoid every harmful substance, but we can consciously opt to consume less of them. This begins with recognizing their detrimental effects and understanding that better options exist, such as cooking with healthy animal fats like ghee, duck fat, pork lard, or beef tallow.

A nutritionist I recently spoke with suggested thinking of fats as good, bad, and ugly. The "ugly" fats, like vegetable and seed oils, should be completely eliminated from our diets.

Now, you may be thinking that olive and avocado oils are the healthiest oils, and you'd be right. Olive oil, high in heart-healthy polyphenols, can be beneficial in combating heart disease. However, these benefits are lost when we cook with these oils at high temperatures. Hence, they're best consumed raw, perhaps in salad dressings. Coconut oil is also fantastic, particularly for brain health, though due to its strong flavor, it's best used in desserts.

Sautéing with Ghee: An Alternative to Vegetable and Seed Oils

Understanding the drawbacks of cooking with vegetable or seed oils, one may wonder what could serve as an appropriate substitute, particularly for sautéing vegetables. The answer, intriguingly, lies in an ancient form of clarified butter known as ghee.

When I first began researching healthier fats for cooking, I found myself revisiting a favorite recipe of mine: sautéed mushrooms in butter. I asked myself what I could use instead of regular butter, and there, in that moment of culinary curiosity, I found ghee.

Ghee has its roots in traditional Indian cooking and is a form of clarified butter, meaning the milk constituents – lactose and casein, which are often the problematic components – have been removed. As a result, ghee becomes a highly saturated fat that not only tastes delicious but is also replete with Conjugated Linoleic Acids (CLA) when derived from organic grass-fed animals. CLAs are purported to possess strong anti-cancer properties, further bolstering the case for ghee as an ideal fat for sautéing vegetables and mushrooms.

Choosing High-Quality, Toxin-Free Animal Fat

When it comes to selecting fats for cooking, quality is paramount. This entails using fats from grass-fed or pasture-raised animals to ensure they're toxin-free. Understandably, concerns may arise due to the supplements, vaccines, antibiotics, hormones, genetically modified organism (GMO) grains, and other substances mass-produced animals are fed. These toxins can accumulate in the animal's fat, causing potential health issues when consumed.

You may not find organic lard readily available at your local health food store, but animal fats, despite their tainted reputation, can be surprisingly affordable, especially those from organically raised animals. Simply pay a visit to your organic butcher and inquire about duck fat, pork lard, beef tallow, and so forth.

Rendering Animal Fat: A Simple Process

Rendering animal fat is a straightforward process, even though it may require a bit of work. Essentially, rendering involves slowly cooking the fat out of meat, which separates the pure fat. An example of this process is rendering bacon, which results in leftover bacon fat that can be used for cooking.

The process of rendering involves trimming any veins, meat, or blood from the piece of fat, then chopping it into small chunks. You then slow cook these fat chunks over low heat for an extended period (generally between 2-8 hours). Once the white fat chunks have turned brown and dry, you strain off the pure fat and let it cool. Once cooled, it solidifies at room temperature and is ready for use in cooking.

Approaching Nutrition with a Scientific Mind

The principles advocated in this book stem from a scientific approach to optimal living and nutrition, challenging longstanding misconceptions. Take a 30-day experiment: replace vegetable or seed oils with animal fats and avoid processed foods high in Omega-6 oils. Observe how your body responds, as each person is unique. However, it's important to consider food allergies. Despite pH balance, some individuals may have intolerances leading to issues like swelling, itching, acne, or weight gain. An elimination diet can help identify these allergies by systematically removing and reintroducing specific foods or groups, enabling informed dietary decisions and optimal well-being.

Food allergies can also be tied to emotional shocks

Dr. Hamer posits that we can develop specific food allergies if we're consuming a food or substance when we receive shocking news. Therefore, overcoming emotional trauma and addressing the root cause, potentially with the aid of Biomagnetism, might help subside the allergies.

Dr. Goiz, our biomagnetic professor, affirmed that if we weren't born with our health obstacle then we can overcome it. This captures the essence of why I'm so passionate about Biomagnetism. I hope this passion resonates with you.

Chapter 15

The Amazing Power of Fruits, Vegetables, Nuts and Seeds

"Let food be thy medicine and medicine be thy food."

– HIPPOCRATES

Throughout history, many cultures have recognized the importance of consuming fruits, vegetables, nuts, and seeds not only for survival but also for maintaining health and treating diseases. However, in today's world, with the rise in obesity and diet-related illnesses, it's evident that humanity as a whole has forgotten the significance of real food. Real food refers to food that is derived from the earth, untouched by chemical alterations and industrial processing for long shelf life in supermarkets.

Real food, such as fruits, vegetables, nuts, and seeds, offers numerous benefits. They are incredibly nutritious, providing essential vitamins, minerals, phytonutrients, fiber, and healthy oils. By understanding the chemical components of these foods, we gain awareness and control over our health. Unfortunately, we have been bombarded with conflicting information about what to eat and what to avoid. This confusion has led to the indiscriminate consumption of supplements, artificially flavored chewing gum, and processed foods – which should probably not even be referred to as "food" – like chips and soda.

Speaking of dairy products, it's crucial to address the issue of milk (lactose) and its potential harm. Pediatric surgeon Dr. Guillermo Pinzon has highlighted the detrimental effects of consuming milk products. Humans are the only species that consume milk from another animal, which is biologically incorrect. The notion that milk is a perfect source of calcium is a myth. In fact, milk is a poor source of calcium compared to other foods. Moreover, the proteins in cow's milk are incompatible with our bodies, forming a polymer (plastic-like) substance when mixed with acids and yeast of our digestive tract. Eliminating milk products from one's diet can lead to remarkable improvements in health, such as increased energy, weight loss, and reduced phlegm production.

Understanding the power of food for nutrition and healing is essential. There is a vast array of food available worldwide, yet we have limited ourselves to a narrow range of options. Many people suffer from malnutrition due to the consumption of pH and nutritionally unbalanced meals. By harnessing the power of food strategically, we can nourish and heal our bodies. The best part is that real foods like vegetables, fruits, nuts, and seeds are often more affordable than medications or supplements.

Looking back at history, we can find fascinating examples of how different cultures used food for medicinal purposes. The Native American culture utilized chocolate to break fevers, while ancient

Greeks turned to carrots to soothe upset stomachs. The Aztecs believed avocados to be nature's Viagra. Real foods have incredible health benefits, and by incorporating them into our diets, we can experience their remarkable effects.

However, it's important to eliminate processed foods and junk foods from our diets as they are very likely causing us more harm than good. These foods contribute to the obesity epidemic and various health problems. The prevalence of junk food in our surroundings makes it challenging to maintain a healthy diet, but it's crucial to prioritize our well-being over temporary indulgence.

To inspire you, let's take a closer look at some common fruits and vegetables and their health benefits:

- **Asparagus:** Low in calories, high in protein, antioxidants, vitamins (A, B6, C, K), and minerals. Helps balance acidity in the body, aids digestion, and has been used to heal arthritis and strengthen the kidneys.

- **Avocados:** Rich in protein, luteins, phytochemicals, and glutathione. They have demonstrated anticancer properties, promote eye health, and are considered an aphrodisiac.

- **Bananas:** Fight depression, improve brain function, relieve hangovers, alleviate morning sickness, and regulate blood pressure. High in potassium, vitamin B6, vitamin C, manganese, and fiber.

- **Beets:** Sweet, tasty, high in minerals (calcium, iron, potassium), and a good source of folate. Stimulate liver function, act as a blood purifier, and contain antioxidants. Calming effect on the body.

- **Broccoli:** A cruciferous vegetable with amazing anticancer properties. High in vitamin C, E, and beta-carotene.

- **Brussels Sprouts:** Similar to other cruciferous vegetables, they are rich in fiber, antioxidants, vitamin C, and promote overall health.

- **Carrots:** Crunchy and delicious, they support liver health, promote eye health, and contain beneficial compounds that fight against macular degeneration and cataracts.

- **Celery:** A natural source of electrolytes, it acts as a natural tranquilizer for insomniacs.

- **Chard:** Low in calories, an excellent source of vitamins (C, K, A, B complex), minerals (calcium, copper, sodium, potassium), and fiber. Can be boiled, steamed, or roasted.

- **Cherries:** Aid in fighting belly fat and post-workout soreness, reduce the risk of stroke, improve sleep patterns, and offer antioxidants, potassium, and vitamins A, C, and iron.

- **Cranberries:** Known for their medicinal qualities, they help fight urinary tract infections.

- **Cucumbers:** High in silica, which strengthens connective tissues.

These are just a few examples, but there are many more fruits and vegetables with incredible health benefits.

In addition to fruits and vegetables, nuts and seeds play a vital role in our diet. They are nutritious, delicious, and complement any meal. Nuts and seeds are high in protein, healthy oils (like omega-3s), vitamins (such as B vitamins), and essential minerals. Despite their high-fat content, they offer numerous health benefits, such as aiding in weight loss, promoting cardiovascular health, and providing antioxidants.

Here are some popular nuts and seeds and their benefits:

- **Almonds:** High in fiber, calcium, vitamin E, magnesium, and selenium. They help you feel full longer.

- **Brazil Nuts:** Good source of monounsaturated fat, selenium, and antioxidants.

- **Cashews:** Rich in folate, vitamin K, and contain tryptophan, which can have mood-enhancing effects.

- **Hazelnuts:** Good source of monounsaturated fat, vitamin E, and promote healthy skin and vision.

- **Macadamia Nuts:** High in monounsaturated fat, vitamins (A, E, B1, B2, B3), and minerals like thiamine and iron.

- **Peanuts:** Good source of monounsaturated fat, vitamin E, and magnesium.

- **Pecans:** Rich in antioxidants, zinc, and provide various essential vitamins and minerals. Good for heart health, healthy skin, and vision.

- **Pine Nuts:** Packed with vitamins (E, K, B1, B2, B3), minerals, protein, and fiber. They have a nutty flavor and can be sprinkled on various dishes.

- **Pistachios:** Aid in weight management, promote heart health, and contain antioxidants, potassium, vitamin B6, and gamma-tocopherol.

- **Walnuts:** Contain melatonin, which aids in sleep, are high in fiber, magnesium, and alpha-linolenic acid (Omega-3 fatty acid).

Seeds also offer a wide range of nutritional benefits:

- **Chia Seeds:** High in Omega-3 fatty acids, fiber, and can aid in weight loss and blood sugar control.

- **Flaxseeds:** High in Omega-3 fatty acids and help reduce inflammation. Best consumed when ground.

- **Hemp Seeds:** Provide essential amino acids, fatty acids, minerals, and vitamins. Great for a well-rounded diet.

- **Pumpkin Seeds:** High in zinc, magnesium, and fiber. Can help regulate blood sugar and provide various health benefits.

- **Sesame Seeds:** Packed with minerals (manganese, copper, calcium, magnesium, iron) and vitamins (B1, E), and provide dietary fiber.

- **Sunflower Seeds:** High in protein, heart-healthy monounsaturated fat, vitamin E, and minerals. Beneficial for overall health.

Incorporating these fruits, vegetables, nuts, and seeds into your diet can provide a wide range of health benefits. Juicing is an excellent way to increase your intake of fruits and vegetables, providing a convenient and nutritious option. By juicing, you can easily consume the recommended daily servings and absorb the nutrients more efficiently. However, remember to include protein and fat in your diet for a balanced nutrition.

Whether you choose to consume organic or non-organic foods, it's important to be mindful of the ingestion of pesticides and hormones from non-organic sources. While organic foods are preferable, accessibility and cost can sometimes be a challenge. To minimize pesticide consumption in non-organic produce, you can soak fruits and vegetables in a solution of filtered water and vinegar for a few minutes.

Remember, the power of real food lies in its ability to nourish and heal our bodies. By incorporating a variety of fruits, vegetables, nuts, and seeds into our diet, we can take control of our health, improve our overall well-being, and enjoy the many benefits of eating real food.

Chapter 16

Exploring Natural Alternatives in the Fight Against Cancer

"Diseases of the soul are more dangerous and more numerous than those of the body."

– CICERO

Cancer stands as the second leading cause of mortality in the United States, claiming over half a million lives annually. On a daily basis, countless individuals are faced with the daunting words from their doctors: "You have cancer."

Typically, the ensuing conversation includes an overview of four treatment options – chemotherapy, radiotherapy, hormone therapy, and surgery – with an urgent reminder that delay might prove fatal. The doctor might even say something along the lines of: "It's either the chemotherapy or the cancer, but at least with treatment, there's a chance."

Fear, a natural reaction in such circumstances, can cloud rational decision-making, leading many patients to acquiesce to the prescribed treatment plan. Unfortunately, it's not uncommon for patients to discover that the treatment's side effects are as debilitating as the disease itself. However, there's a growing trend of individuals opting for safe and natural alternatives, often with significant success, before resorting to allopathic cancer therapies.

For various reasons, whether financial, political, or simply ignorance, doctors often fail to mention these natural options which are proving successful for many. Consider, for example, the research documented in The China Study by T. Colin Campbell, PhD, and Thomas M. Campbell II, MD. Their extensive study suggests that by adjusting one's diet to include 25% animal protein and 75% plant protein, certain cancers and diabetes can be cured. Moreover, this dietary shift has also been associated with the reversal of arthritis and other degenerative health conditions. But the truth is that this nutritional conversation goes deeper than this, but also requires understanding the things that kill our microbiome that contribute to disease.

Dr. Hamer's research also provides an emotional perspective on cancer. He posits that sudden, distressing emotional events can precipitate the onset of cancers and other chronic degenerative disease. Dr. Hamer's therapeutic approach focuses on verbal counseling, and despite controversy, his methods have shown unexpectedly high cancer survival rates in documented cases.

His work indicates that when individuals successfully confront, reconcile with, or resolve traumatic experiences – thus neutralizing the emotional conflict – the body can begin its healing process. This concept underscores the importance of introspection and dealing with traumatic experiences head-on, regardless of when they occurred. If a particular incident still causes discomfort when you try to speak about it, it's a sign that it continues to impact your life.

Conventional Medicine Treatment

Within the realm of conventional medicine, there exists a considerable debate over cancer diagnosis and treatment methodologies. For instance, while one pathologist might interpret a test result as indicative of cancer, another could conclude the opposite. Similarly, while one physician might immediately recommend treatments like surgery, chemotherapy, radiation, or hormone therapy, another might suggest a wait-and-see approach.

There's currently a contentious discussion within the medical community concerning the issue of overtreatment. In recent years, there has been a notable shift towards recommending fewer cancer screenings. The primary reason for this shift is the realization that aggressive treatment and testing regimens do not necessarily enhance patients' quality of life. Indeed, in many instances, patients find that the prescribed treatments can be more taxing than the disease itself, attacking the body's ability to heal or control the disease naturally.

This predicament underscores the fundamental disparity between allopathic and holistic approaches. Holistic or natural medicine aims to empower the mind, body, and spirit, fostering the body's innate healing capacities. On the contrary, allopathic medicine typically employs pharmaceutical and surgical means to kill or extract harmful germs or cells, inevitably affecting the beneficial ones in the process.

With a plethora of opinions, experiences, and backgrounds, it can be overwhelming to navigate the healthcare landscape. The looming fear of mortality further complicates the decision-making process, often sidelining solid research-based choices.

Many individuals place their complete trust in doctors, failing to realize that physicians, while highly trained, possess a specific set of skills that most likely does not consider alternative methods, particularly natural ones.

It's essential to recognize that conventional medicine doesn't hold all the answers, but let's also be clear and honest that nobody on earth holds all the answers. Evidence of this fact can be found in the increasing number of people suffering from diseases and the growing number of tombstones in the cemeteries despite using pharmaceutical drugs, surgeries and natural modalities.

What Triggers Cancer?

The reality is that allopathic medicine does not fully understand the underlying causes of cancer. There are several potential contributing factors, including:

1. Consumption of "foods" high in sugar and calories but low in nutrients creating detrimental effects on our microbiome.

2. Exposure to harmful substances, such as medicinal drugs, tobacco, and various chemicals found in food (i.e. preservatives, artificial sweeteners), air, and water, including pesticides and synthetic hormones in non-organic meat and dairy products, and more.

3. Prolonged exposure to electromagnetic fields from appliances, cell phones, computers, TVs, and microwaves.

4. Genetic predisposition.

In the face of a cancer diagnosis, when people seek understanding and solutions, it can be deeply disconcerting to find that conventional medicine may not provide satisfactory answers. Despite this reality, many people repeatedly turn to this system for help at the first sign of discomfort.

A personal story illuminates this. I once received a call from someone suffering from a persistent urinary infection. Despite several changes in prescription, the antibiotics prescribed by his doctor weren't helping. While I had successfully helped him with an unrelated issue years earlier, he did not think to seek my assistance sooner. This anecdote exemplifies our instinctive reliance on conventional medicine, even when it may not always provide the best solutions. But the great news is that after Biomagnetism, the infection was gone.

Dr. Goiz' Cancer Code

According to Dr. Goiz, the formation of a benign tumor, or neoplasia, requires the presence of three bacterial infections and one virus. If your doctor tells you not to worry because your tumor is non-cancerous, it's nonetheless a situation that warrants attention.

Worrying is counterproductive. Instead, self-education, such as you are doing by reading this book, and immediate action, using Biomagnetic methods and lifestyle changes, should be the response.

In comparing benign and malignant tumors, Dr. Goiz's research suggests that their formation process isn't significantly different. The key factor in transforming a benign tumor into a malignant one is the presence of a specific bacterium – Mycobacterium leprae.

Cancer can affect various body parts, such as the skin, muscles, liver, pancreas, stomach, etc., and its progression can vary wildly from one person to another. Dr. Goiz explains that when a fungal infection is added to the basic cancer-causing components, the cancer can progress rapidly. The presence of a parasitic infection, on the other hand, can lead to metastasis or even necrosis.

Dr. Goiz's Biomagnetism Therapy

The unique aspect of Dr. Goiz's method is its recognition that all infections, dysfunctions, emotions, toxins, and more cause specific biochemical imbalances in the body. With the utilization of magnetic fields, these imbalances can be identified and corrected, thereby promoting optimal health and improved quality of life. This approach has not only been utilized for prevention and improvement of various conditions, but has also been life-saving within our biomagnetic field.

Interestingly, these imbalances can be detected before any physical signs or symptoms emerge. Consider, for example, a person who believes they are naturally bad-tempered. In actuality, this could be an emotional defense mechanism, and identifying such a blocked emotion could lead to profound transformation.

From a biomagnetic viewpoint, the root causes of all diseases, such as cancer, arthritis, diabetes, multiple sclerosis, fibromyalgia, and more, are understood from a biochemical and energetic perspective. Therefore, not only is Biomagnetism safe, powerful, precise, and efficient when dealing with health issues, it's also an essential part of a balanced lifestyle.

Adopting a balanced lifestyle will most likely prevent long periods of sickness. Short-term illness is common, but when it stretches into weeks or months, or repeatedly occurs throughout the years, it's a clear indication of an underlying imbalance.

The scientific understanding of Dr. Goiz is increasingly being validated over time through countless testimonials from individuals who were previously told they had no other option but to wait for death or learn to live with pain. As practitioners of Medical Pair Biomagnetism, we are consistently witnessing effective healing results, not just for cancer, but for numerous other diseases that are believed to have no natural solution.

Dr. Goiz spent over 30 years championing this revolutionary discovery, which requires substantial courage and dedication. He always advised us, his students, to aid people using this method, but to remain silent to avoid the persecution he has faced.

However, if we were to remain silent, we would be complicit in the world's wrongs and wouldn't be serving humanity, which is the motivation behind this book. This approach has the potential to save lives, including those of future great leaders. Consider, for instance, the following case.

In March of 2012, I received a call regarding a 12-year-old girl diagnosed with brain cancer at the age of eight. Despite undergoing brain surgery and four years of chemotherapy, the tumor continued to grow. Doctors were unwilling to perform additional surgery due to high risk, and her mother was desperate to try an alternative approach as they were told that her survival was unlikely.

When I first met the girl, she was resentful at being brought in. She shouted at me, "You're not a real doctor and I'm tired of promises that aren't true." In that moment, I realized I needed to treat her with respect and understand that she needed to be part of the decision-making process. I told her, "I completely understand your frustration and if I was in your shoes I'd feel the same way. I want it to be your decision, so if you want to leave right now that's okay with me..." After a few moments of silence, she agreed to proceed with the treatment.

Immediately after the magnets were placed on her body, she felt a strange sensation. After about 20 minutes with the magnets, she fell asleep and, upon waking, she said, "I want to come back tomorrow." Within one month her tumor size decreased significantly despite discontinuing chemotherapy, and over the following six months, it was completely gone. The surprising thing is that we only did about 6 sessions in that time span.

The secrecy around Biomagnetism

Patients often choose not to share with their doctors that they are trying alternative therapies, as was the case with the family of the child just mentioned. It can be challenging to have an open and honest discussion with physicians who are unfamiliar with Medical Pair Biomagnetism and tend to be skeptical about natural treatments. However, despite the risk of being criticized or dismissed by doctors, it's essential to share these experiences. After all, doctors are people too, with their own families and health concerns.

What if one doctor witnessed a miraculous recovery and decided to explore Biomagnetism further, integrating it into their practice and collaborating with biomagnetic therapists? This could potentially bridge the gap between different healthcare options and alleviate the confusion people often face when deciding on the best healthcare approach.

Preventing Mastectomy through Biomagnetism

I have had the opportunity to aid women in eliminating breast tumors, thus circumventing the need for mastectomy. One such instance involved a woman who was due for a mastectomy in a month. After undergoing two sessions of biomagnetic therapy at our healing center, she returned to the hospital for her surgery. To everyone's surprise, there was no tumor to be found.

When questioned by her medical team, she chose to remain silent about her biomagnetic therapy, fearing it might land me in trouble. This patient was immediately discharged from the hospital. While these stories of recovery might seem uncommon, they occur more often than you might think.

However, it's essential to be proactive rather than reactive when it comes to your health. Delaying the use of Medical Biomagnetism and allowing disease progression could hinder complete recovery. Regular body recalibration and a healthy lifestyle are critical.

Goizean Theory on Cysts and Polyps

Many patients are told by their doctors that their diagnosed cysts may turn cancerous. Although there's some truth to it as cysts often involve infections, this doesn't mean it's an inevitable progression.

According to Dr. Goiz, cysts and polyps occur due to a symbiotic relationship between a bacterial and a viral infection. A patient I had worked with previously reported that her uterine cysts had disappeared by her annual check-up. The doctor's disbelief at this development reflects the medical field's reluctance to accept the potential for natural healing from cysts.

Stories like these aren't isolated incidents. My colleagues and I, who practice Dr. Goiz's biomagnetic method, have consistently seen favorable results with conditions such as fibroids, cysts, and tumors, which are often deemed incurable and are managed with medication and surgery.

Medications Falling Short

When health issues stem from infections, why do medications sometimes fail? While antibiotics were once heralded as miracle cures, the medical field now faces dwindling treatment options. Dr. Goiz attributes this to the overuse of medicinal resources, including vaccinations, antivirals, and antibiotics.

Dr. Goiz likens the shift in bacterial and viral behavior to an abused child growing up to become aggressive. Similarly, as bacteria and viruses adapt, there is a mounting need for stronger medications to combat these evolved pathogens.

Dr. Goiz's Perspective on disease and healing

According to Dr. Goiz, barring physical trauma and congenital birth defects, nearly 98% of all diseases or health issues are potentially curable, provided you act before irreversible tissue damage occurs. In simpler terms, if a condition is not congenital, it can be healed. However, if you wait until you lose sight, chances are you won't regain it.

By comprehending the causes of diseases like cancer, we can better understand other health challenges. Dr. Goiz maintains that no single factor – be it a virus, bacteria, fungus, parasite, dysfunction, or emotional trauma – can solely lead to chronic degenerative disease.

Disease usually manifests when there are two or more factors disturbing the body's pH balance. These factors could include multiple germs, a combination of germs and dysfunctions, two or more dysfunctions, or multiple emotional traumas. Essentially, disease arises from two or more pH-altering factors.

Consider conditions like arthritis, multiple sclerosis, fibromyalgia, and lupus. Often, the diagnosis does not indicate the root-cause; instead, it offers a description of a degenerative process. Labeling joint inflammation as arthritis and accepting it as incurable and manageable only through medication is unacceptable. There are identifiable origins to arthritis and other health conditions.

So, if medical professionals claim there's no cure for such conditions, why do people experience improvement and healing after undergoing Medical Pair Biomagnetism?

The answer is straightforward. Restoring the body's pH balance with Biomagnetism, along with proper nutrition, positive mindset, gratitude, self-love, and peace, promotes a well-functioning body and life. With this understanding and proactive action, a healthy life becomes an achievable goal.

Durazo's vision for humanity

While writing the first edition of my book, *Biomagnetism: The Mind, Body, Spirit Recalibration System,* I was aware that I might face criticism and accusations of promoting pseudoscience or placebo effect. Despite this, I felt compelled to share the knowledge that had benefited those close to me, believing it could help others too.

I envisioned a world where everyone could experience the benefits of Biomagnetism firsthand; hence, I created a self-help guide. I wanted to demonstrate that Biomagnetism could offer benefits without the risks of injury or addiction, using this safe, natural energy.

My aim was to provide people with magnets and simple-to-follow strategies, showing them a simple way to alleviate pain and enhance their quality of life, thereby inviting them to embrace this transformative science. The goal was to guide people to their optimal selves, and their warm responses confirmed that I was on the right path. This prompted me to substantially revise this edition and include even more information about living an optimal life.

Chapter 17

Key Considerations Before Vaccination

'We drink one another's health and spoil our own."
– JEROME K. JEROME

In our modern world, where information is abundant and often conflicting, the journey towards optimal health can be challenging. The vast quantity of available data, along with the prevalence of censorship, adds to the complexity. To make well-informed choices that enhance our well-being and that of our loved ones, it's essential to remain informed.

It's not good enough to make choices based solely on personal feelings or external pressures. For example, just because I've avoided all pharmaceuticals since I was 18 years old, doesn't mean you should too. Because I have informed myself and learned specialized medical skills, this way-of-life suits my circumstances. The primary aim of this book is to present you with traditional medicine and well-researched information, allowing you to live your healthiest life in a way that is safe and minimizes the risks of unnecessary suffering.

The essence of living a healthy life requires a dedication to staying current with trustworthy, evidence-based, honest, and transparent sources. This on-going commitment to knowledge-seeking is super important to enhancing and maintaining our quality of life.

Understanding the big issues surrounding vaccinations is vital, as they interact with our body's natural defenses against infections in ways that are often not fully acknowledged. While our innate immune system is equipped with various mechanisms to detoxify infectious agents – including the skin, respiratory cells, stomach pH, and liver-initiated detoxification systems – vaccinations introduce a different dynamic. By bypassing three out of these four primary detox pathways, vaccines present a unique challenge to the liver, as their ingredients are delivered directly into the bloodstream and potentially affect every organ they encounter.

Furthermore, it's essential to consider the impact of vaccines on the immune system itself. We are born with a natural immune system designed to protect us. However, emerging studies suggest that vaccinated individuals might experience a weakening of this system. This aspect raises concerns about the long-term consequences of vaccines, particularly regarding the body's ability to naturally resist and recover from infections.

No matter how difficult this conversation may seem, being well-informed about the components and effects of commonly used vaccines is crucial for making educated choices about whether to vaccinate yourself and your family. Such informed decisions are key to preventing potential regrets in the future. This chapter aims to explore these lesser-known aspects of vaccines, which have been overlooked for years. Our commitment to truth, transparency, and the safeguarding of educational rights and health is reflected in our carefully selected sources for this book.

Here is an overview of four esteemed organizations that I invite you to follow:

1. **Informed Consent Action Network (ICAN):** ICAN, a nonprofit organization founded by Del Bigtree, producer of documentaries like "Vaxxed: From Cover-Up to Catastrophe," focuses on informed consent in medical treatments and vaccine safety. They employ the Freedom of Information Act (FOIA) to secure the truth from government agencies and are dedicated to funding scientific studies into the causes of manmade diseases. Websites: https://icandecide.org | https://thehighwire.com/

2. **Children's Health Defense (CHD):** Founded by Robert F. Kennedy, Jr., CHD aims to end chronic childhood diseases, hold responsible parties accountable, and challenge governments, corporations, and regulatory agencies. They advocate for issues related to children's health and provide information on various topics, including vaccination. Website: https://childrenshealthdefense.org/

3. **America's Frontline Doctors (AFLDS):** AFLDS was formed by healthcare professionals who observed interference with medical freedom and civil liberties during the COVID-19 pandemic. They advocate for science-based facts about the pandemic, oppose medical cancel culture and censorship, and seek to protect Constitutional rights. Website: https://americasfrontlinedoctors.org/

4. **Protection of the Educational Rights of Kids (PERK):**
    PERK is a nonprofit organization committed to safeguarding educational rights for children, defending medical liberties, and opposing vaccine mandates and policies. They also support service members who refuse the COVID-19 vaccine. Website: https://www.perk-group.com

In the midst of the information flood, making informed health decisions can feel like a daunting journey. The pursuit of knowledge becomes super urgent, especially when loved ones experience adverse reactions following vaccination. For some, this realization arrives tragically late, in instances where vaccination is directly linked to a loved one's death. However, by utilizing resources from these reputable organizations dedicated to truth, transparency, educational rights and health protection, you can uncover factual information, grasp scientific studies, and gain confidence in the accuracy of your knowledge. This is crucial because you want to be well-informed before making pharmaceutical decisions that could potentially hurt your health, maybe even permanently, instead of promoting well-being.

These organizations are a great resource for you, as they collectively challenge the status quo and advocate for the pursuit of truth and transparency in health and vaccination. In this chapter I'll provide a comprehensive perspective on vaccination-related issues, empowering you to make informed choices regarding health, safety, and individual rights. Your knowledge will become your power as you stand firm in your commitment to truth and the well-being of your family.

How Medical Freedom Affects You

In the past, medical freedom and informed consent may not have been at the forefront of your concerns. However, the events of the COVID-19 pandemic have brought these issues into the spotlight, prompting many to question various aspects of medical decision-making, and rightly so.

During the COVID pandemic, or "Scamdemic," as one of my physician friends calls it, people found themselves asking:

- "Why am I required to take the vaccine to maintain my job?"

- "Is it fair for my family to be quarantined in another country due to exposure, incurring significant expenses?"

- "Will my children be subjected to vaccination in school without my consent?"

- "Why is mask-wearing mandated in every store, and why do I experience skin issues after prolonged use?"

- "Do I really need to take the vaccine when COVID-19 has a survival rate of over 99%?"

These questions are fundamentally about medical freedom and informed consent, and they extend beyond the pandemic. There are various situations where your rights regarding medical decisions can be at risk:

1. **Mental Health Treatments:** When you're not allowed to make decisions about your mental health treatments, including medication, therapy, and hospitalization before they are administered.

2. **Genetic Testing:** When you aren't consulted about genetic testing to discover your genetic predispositions and risk factors for certain health conditions.

3. **End-of-Life Decisions:** At the end of your life, when you're told that it would be best to start making arrangements to die and that you'll be assisted with this decision.

4. **Deficient Informed Consent:** When certain medical treatments and procedures are initiated without providing you with all the necessary information about the risks, benefits, and alternatives.

5. **Limited Options:** When your medical team insists that there are no alternative options for you, dismissing alternative health advice as misinformation.

6. **Clinical Trials:** When you discover later that your doctor conducted a clinical trial with you as a subject without your consent.

7. **Research Studies:** When you enroll in a study without complete disclosure of the study's objectives and potential risks.

In these situations, it's crucial to ask questions – you have every right to seek answers and make informed decisions that align with your personal values. It's important to remember that medical professionals are NOT God, nor are they law enforcement, despite some individuals assuming the context of such roles. Failing to inquire, simply because you assume they know better, can lead to the erosion of your rights and medical freedom.

Furthermore, keep in mind that there are diverse paths to achieving well-being. Even within the same field of allopathic medicine, you may encounter various medical opinions. Maybe you haven't personally faced these issues yet, but understanding these concepts empowers you to identify potential violations of your rights before any harm occurs. Empowerment is the primary objective of providing you with this book. Also, remember that learning should be a continuous process.

In this chapter, we must explore issues around vaccine production, licensing, ethical considerations, adverse effects, and historical insights related to medical freedom and informed consent. With this broader perspective, you'll gain insight into why some individuals adopted a so-called "anti-vax" stance during the pandemic. We were a little less than half of the population who were very *well-informed*, not only about the power of our innate ability to heal, but about the facts and ethical principles at play.

Unfortunately, many people only realized the importance of advocating for their health and being cautious about vaccinations after they or their family members had already received the vaccine – but even then, it's better late than never. They experienced firsthand the detrimental consequences, offering them a front-row view of what was truly transpiring behind the scenes.

Let's explore three key aspects of vaccinations:

1. Aborted Fetal Tissue and DNA Contamination

2. The Lack of Comprehensive Testing

3. Flawed Vaccine Testing and Placebos

Aborted Fetal Tissue and DNA Contamination

You may find it hard to believe that vaccines were developed with aborted fetal tissue, but this unsettling reality has been a recurring practice. Dr. Stanley Plotkin, a prominent vaccine authority, once testified under oath that he couldn't recall the exact number of times aborted fetal tissue was used in vaccines but admitted to "quite a few" instances. Shockingly, company documents revealed that 76 fetuses, three months or older, and in "good health", were used in a single study. Various tissues, including pituitary glands, kidneys, spleens, hearts, tongues, and lungs, were harvested for vaccine culture.

The process is to use fetal cells to grow viruses. The truth is that vaccines have been made using fetal cells for a long time, and this information has been kept from the public. Some of the vaccines that use these cells include the rubella, chickenpox, hepatitis A, and rabies vaccines. During the pandemic, some COVID-19 vaccines, like AstraZeneca (UK), Johnson & Johnson (U.S.A), and CanSino Biologics (China), employed fetal tissue in their development. Manufacturers argue that the final vaccine product is "purified" of fetal cells and does not contain them.

This raises ethical concerns, as it hints at the use of human life as a commodity. From a religious and spiritual perspective, this practice raises ethical dilemmas related to the sanctity of life and the moral implications of utilizing murdered fetal cells for medical purposes. It prompts a profound reflection on the values associated with trading murder (abortion) for supposed health and immunity, which by the way was promised, however, turned out to be false.

The concept of spiritual balance highlights the importance of maintaining a righteous and ethical stance in all interactions and decisions, whether with God, nature, or healthcare agencies. This notion reminds us that choices made in these areas can have profound spiritual and moral weight, needing a careful balance between spiritual obligations, healthcare needs, and ethical principles.

Integrating into this discussion is the critical question of trust in healthcare practitioners, particularly when their professional autonomy appears constrained. Often, these professionals face a stark choice: adhere strictly to vaccination guidelines as dictated by their employers or government agencies, or risk their careers. This predicament raises concerns about the authenticity and independence of their advice. Are these practitioners truly free to exercise medical judgment, or are they compelled to follow predetermined protocols, potentially at the expense of individual patient needs? The evidence points to the latter.

This dilemma is relevant considering the accusation that some healthcare practitioners are merely echoing agenda-driven narratives from government bodies, rather than basing their recommendations on sound science and common sense. Research has shown that healthcare professionals often promote vaccines based on personal beliefs rather than robust medical evidence affirming their safety. Moreover, studies suggest that a more effective method to influence parental decisions regarding vaccinations is through discussions about the decision-making process rather than proving additional medical data. This revelation points to why many continue to feel forced to vaccinate against their wishes, and it begs the question of how much trust can be placed in their counsel.

Animal Cell Alternatives

While some regulatory agencies claim to oversee fetal tissue use in vaccine production, concerns remain. Consider the alternatives to fetal tissue used in vaccines, which still raise concerns. These alternatives include animal cell lines and synthetic cell lines, which may introduce DNA contamination or unforeseen issues. Once foreign DNA becomes integrated into an organism's cellular DNA, according to scientific consensus, it cannot return to its original state, potentially affecting biological processes, causing mutations, altering gene expression, and even leading to chronic health conditions or cancer. This concern is further fueled by the discovery of DNA fragments in mRNA COVID-19 vaccines.

A significant concern regarding vaccines is whether DNA fragments become integrated into the recipient's DNA. While studies have confirmed the presence of DNA fragments from vaccines in the bloodstream, the critical question remains: do these fragments become integrated into the recipient's DNA, potentially altering their genetic makeup and humanity? The short answer is yes. According to The Epoch Times, the DNA fragments in Pfizer and Moderna vaccines exceeded the FDA's 10 ng/dose requirements, but Pfizer never disclosed this information to the public.

Instances of foreign DNA contamination in vaccines have arisen before. In the late 1990s, rotavirus vaccine batches were found to be contaminated with Bovine Viral Diarrhea Virus (BVDV), leading to a temporary withdrawal of the vaccine from the market. However, in the case of COVID-19 vaccines, they were swiftly brought to market without the opportunity for thorough contamination checks. Now, three to four years down the line, it's evident that the consequences are irreversible. The harm has already taken its toll.

The Lack of Comprehensive Testing

The issue of comprehensive testing, or the lack thereof, in the context of vaccinations is a matter of great concern for public health and informed decision-making. Comprehensive studies, particularly those comparing vaccinated individuals with their unvaccinated counterparts, play a pivotal role in assessing vaccine safety and efficacy, but why are they not being conducted?

Let's look at some of the reasons:

1. **Ethical Concerns:** The medical community often raises ethical concerns about deliberately withholding vaccines from groups of people. While withholding vaccines from individuals is a sensitive matter, many in the public want these studies to be able to make informed decisions about vaccination.

2. **Availability of Unvaccinated Populations:** Finding a sufficient number of unvaccinated individuals for such studies can be challenging, especially if a significant portion of the population is already vaccinated. Governmental agencies sometimes bypass these studies due to the difficulty in locating unvaccinated subjects. In an interview on ICAN, it was revealed that the CDC declined to conduct vaccinated vs. unvaccinated studies for the Measles, Mumps, and Rubella (MMR) vaccination. Initial investigations by a prominent researcher and whistleblower indicated a notably elevated autism risk when this vaccine was administered between the ages of 12-18 months, following the pediatric vaccination schedule, especially among African American boys. Remarkably, when the MMR vaccination was postponed until the child was older than 3 years, the autism rate did not show a significant increase. Unfortunately, the decision not to pursue the vaccinated vs. unvaccinated study omitted this crucial piece of information from the available data, leaving both healthcare professionals and parents without essential insights. The refusal of our own regulatory agencies to conduct these studies raises suspicions and suggests the possibility of undisclosed information hidden from the public eye.

3. **Influence of Other Factors:** Various factors, including individuals' health conditions, access to healthcare, socioeconomic status, and cultural beliefs, can influence vaccine outcomes. Researchers may hesitate to conduct vaxxed vs. unvaxxed studies because these confounding factors could impact the results. For example, any diseases that cause poor immunity may cause either greater reactivity

to vaccines or lessened immunity towards the illness being vaccinated against. Thus, studies have to be comprehensive enough to be able to see if these factors are influencing the results of those who are vaxxed or unvaxxed, and that takes a lot of money.

4. **Study Type:** Some vaccination studies are retrospective, meaning they look back in time to observe associations, which may have limitations.

5. **Funding:** Large-scale, long-term studies are expensive. Funding sources can influence the independence and objectivity of the research. Pharmaceutical companies and private entities often fund CDC studies, and other of our regulatory agencies, raising the obvious concerns about conflicts of interest.

6. **Vaccination vs. Drug Studies:** Vaccination studies differ from drug studies, as vaccines are classified as public health measures. This classification may lead to variations in study design, such as the absence of double-blind, placebo-based, or long-term studies – meaning there is less scrutiny on vaccines licensing. In the case of the MMR, children were receiving six to nine doses per doctor visit. The effects of loading up all these doses were never considered. Similarly, with COVID-19, the studies may not have been isolated to only one vaccine, one brand, and may have been done on those who had multiple doses.

While conducting comprehensive vaxxed vs. unvaxxed studies can be challenging, their benefits are significant. These studies provide insights into how vaccines perform in real-world scenarios among diverse populations, helping identify at-risk groups and assessing long-term and side effects that may not be apparent in initial clinical trials.

While clinical trials offer controlled environments, it's the real-world data that allows us to make more accurate assessments of vaccine efficacy. Rare or long-term side effects may remain hidden until vaccines are administered to a larger and more diverse population over several years. Only through comprehensive, long-term studies involving a substantial number of individuals can we detect unexpected adverse events that may not have surfaced during initial clinical trials.

Transparency in vaccine research fosters trust among the public, healthcare providers, and policymakers. It allows for adjustments in vaccine recommendations, vaccination strategies, and safety monitoring, ultimately aiding in managing outbreaks and emerging variants while building confidence in vaccination programs. Regrettably, our regulatory agencies are failing when it comes to performing these much-needed studies or even acknowledging and following the science when the data is made available by the many prestigious institutions around the world.

Addressing Potential Biases in Vaccine Research: Toward Transparency and Trust

As we continue our path to being informed healthcare consumers, it's crucial for us to scrutinize the details of studies and consider factors like the source of funding and the methodology used when evaluating vaccine-related information. Informed decision-making relies on a comprehensive understanding of the available evidence.

Research in the field of vaccines, like any other scientific endeavor, can be susceptible to biases that impact how results are interpreted and subsequently influence the development of public health policies. The foundation for mitigating these biases lies in transparency, as it allows for a more accurate assessment of the credibility and trustworthiness of vaccine studies.

Some of the potential biases in vaccine research are:

1. **Publication Bias:** One prevalent concern is the selective publication of studies with positive and statistically significant results while withholding those with negative findings. This practice can create a distorted perception of vaccine effectiveness.

2. **Funding Sources:** The source of funding for a study can introduce conflicts of interest and bias into the outcomes. Therefore, understanding who funded a study is essential for evaluating its impartiality.

3. **Selection Bias:** If study participants are not representative of the target population, selection bias may distort the results, limiting their generalizability.

4. **Surveillance Bias:** Differences in how vaccinated and unvaccinated subjects are monitored for adverse events can lead to surveillance bias. An example of this is the 13 HPV vaccine studies called vaxxed vs. unvaxxed. All except for one study with a control group of 17 HIV-positive girls use other vaccines or an injection of the aluminum adjuvant contained in the HPV vaccine as a control. High rates of serious injuries and chronic illness reported by the HPV vaccine recipients were dismissed as not being a vaccine safety issue because the rates were similar to those reported in the "spiked" control group.

5. **Recall Bias:** Surveys or retrospective studies may suffer from recall bias when subjects inaccurately remember or report their vaccination history or adverse events.

6. **Confounding Bias:** Some subjects may have underlying health conditions or exposures to other diseases that can confound study results. Proper study design and statistical analysis can help control for these variables.

7. **Reporting Bias:** Researchers may under- or over report vaccine adverse events, leading to inaccurate assessments of vaccine safety.

8. **Data Manipulation:** Data manipulation, such as cherry-picking data to support a particular outcome or hypothesis, can undermine the integrity of studies.

9. **Biases and Pharmaceutical Companies:** Pharmaceutical companies, driven by financial incentives, may downplay safety concerns to secure licensure, as they bear minimal liability for vaccine injuries. This can erode trust in vaccine research. As explained by Dr. Marcia Angell, currently a professor in the Center for Bioethics, Harvard School of Medicine, and member of the Institute of Medicine, and former editor-in-chief of the New England Journal of Medicine stated, "It is no longer possible to believe much of the clinical research that is published, or to rely on the judgment of trusted physicians or authoritative medical guidelines. I take no pleasure in this conclusion, which I reached slowly and reluctantly over my two decades as an editor of The New England Journal of Medicine."

10. **Timeframes in Studies:** Another critical issue in vaccine studies is the duration of follow-up. In many cases, the follow-up period may not be long enough to detect adverse effects. The developing immune system of newborns, which continues for several years, underscores the need for extended observation periods. Thus, giving a vaccine, which affects the immune system, has the potential to affect that system during the entire time it is developing. Making any decisions on whether or not something has affected vaccine results is premature before the time ends for development. Similarly, the effects on the brain may not be seen until the baby has grown up and is in early adulthood so any study claiming there are no effects is suspicious and even doubtful about the claims made.

Engerix B, the vaccine manufactured by GSK for hepatitis B virus, was originally licensed for children in the late 1980s based on an uncontrolled trial that only reviewed safety for five days. Twenty years later, Engerix B had to be reapproved by HHS after the preservative used in the vaccine was changed. The vaccine otherwise remained identical to what had been approved years prior.

In the reapproval clinical trial report submitted by GSK to HHS in 2005, more than half of the babies reported an adverse event within three days of receiving this vaccine, and 55 of the 587 babies in the study reported a serious adverse event. That means 9.4% of the babies experienced a serious adverse event. Because there wasn't a placebo control group, however, GSK's paid researchers decided that these adverse events were not caused by the vaccine and the vaccine was reapproved.

Flawed Vaccine Testing and Placebos

Scientific studies considered valid typically involve the use of placebos to test the effects of a new substance. Placebos, often in the form of sugar pills, serve to minimize the placebo effect, where a person's condition improves due to the belief in the treatment's effectiveness. This underscores the power of the human mind.

However, vaccines elicit specific responses from the immune system, and selecting an appropriate placebo has been challenging. For nearly all pediatric vaccines promoted by the U.S. Department of Health and Human Services (HHS), clinical trials lack placebo-control groups. This omission questions the confidence in the safety of these vaccines. Unlike drugs like Botox, Prozac, and Lipitor, which undergo placebo-controlled trials, vaccines for children should be subject to the same rigorous evaluation before approval.

New Vaccines Without Any Placebo-Controlled Trial Even When No Vaccine for the Same Disease Exists

In some cases, new vaccines cannot be compared to similar existing vaccines for the same disease, leading to challenges in conducting proper placebo-controlled studies. While this approach may save time and costs, it may compromise public safety.

Scientific rigor dictates preclinical testing in animals, in vitro experiments, and a review of related studies to assess potential risks associated with vaccine ingredients. Comparing a new vaccine with existing ones that share components or mechanisms is another method, although not always appropriate.

In vaccines, adjuvants like aluminum salts enhance immune responses. However, comparing them to similar toxic substances may not provide a fair assessment of safety. Inert placebos like sugar pills or saline injections are essential for unbiased safety evaluations.

Monitoring the Adverse Events after Vaccination

After licensure, vaccines are monitored for adverse events through the Vaccine Adverse Event Reporting System (VAERS). However, VAERS may underreport events significantly, raising concerns about the accuracy of vaccine safety data.

Harvard Medical School found that over a 3-year period at Harvard Pilgrim Health Care, less than 1% of vaccine adverse events were reported. This is significant because in 2016, there were only 59,117 adverse vaccine events reported. Below is a table of more realistic statistics based on this Harvard study:

	VAERS Reports	More Reliable Numbers
Adverse vaccine events	59,117	5,911,700
Deaths	432	43,200
Permanent disabilities	1,091	109,100
Hospitalizations	4,132	413,200
ER visits	10,284	1,028,400

HHS has refused to improve VAERS and will not initiate long-term, inert-placebo controlled trials. Meanwhile, people receiving vaccinations are suffering.

The Implications of Using Vaccines Compared to Other Pharmaceutical Products

Unlike pharmaceutical drugs given to the sick, vaccines are administered to healthy individuals, often children. Therefore, adverse events have broader public health implications. But if adverse events are changing healthy individuals into those who are disabled, then society as a whole is not benefitting.

Drugs that are licensed by the FDA undergo long-term, double-blind clinical trials before they are licensed. During this time, the rate of adverse reactions is under review and compared to the rate of adverse reactions of those in a group receiving an inert placebo such as a sugar pill or saline injection. Even with these long-term studies, drugs are still often recalled.

As mentioned before, vaccines are not required to undergo this same rigorous testing process to assess safety. In fact, not a single one of the clinical trials for vaccines given to babies and toddlers had a control group receiving an inert placebo. Most pediatric vaccines currently on the market have been approved based on studies with inadequate follow-up periods of only up to a few weeks.

Here are a few examples:

1. Merck Hepatitis B vaccines were licensed for injection into one-day-old babies with a *follow-up of five days* after vaccination.

2. GlaxoSmithKline's Hepatitis B vaccines were licensed with a follow-up of only *four days* after vaccination.

3. HiB vaccines were licensed based on trials that solicited adverse reactions for *three to four* days after vaccination.

4. The stand-alone polio vaccine was licensed after a 48-hour follow-up period.

In these trials, either there was no control group at all or the control group received other vaccines as a placebo. This is a flawed study design. The real adverse event rate for a vaccine is determined only by comparing subjects receiving the vaccine with those receiving an inert placebo. There's no pre-licensure safety data and the vaccines are thus assessed for safety only after real world children receive them.

If vaccine testing is flawed and placebos are bad choices, the risk-benefit assessment that is made will potentially lead to inadequate safety evaluations as well as outbreaks and higher incidences of disease. These bad choices may also fail to ensure participant safety and informed consent and/or do not accurately mimic vaccine-induced immune responses, which won't determine the vaccine's true effectiveness. The end result of all this could be not only wasted time and money but ill health for the public.

In the pursuit of transparent and accurate vaccine safety information, it's crucial to rely on reputable sources. Organizations like the Informed Consent Action Network, Children's Health Defense, America's Frontline Doctors, and the Protection of the Educational Rights of Kids have highlighted concerns related to vaccine ethics, safety, and transparency. These valid concerns include the use of placebos, sometimes involving toxic substances, in vaccine trials. Additionally, biases in vaccine testing can introduce uncertainties into safety assessments. Advocating for comprehensive and impartial vaccine safety research is essential for informed decision-making.

Chapter 18

Taking No Action: Hitting the Rock Bottom Method

*"We can only know that we know nothing. And that
is the highest degree of having wisdom."*

– LEO TOLSTOY

When it comes to taking action, choosing to do nothing is still a form of action. I refer to this inaction as hitting rock bottom – a deliberate and systematic plan that leads to physical, emotional, and spiritual suffering. It's intriguing to observe that while people meticulously care for their material possessions, like their cell phones and cars, they often disregard the maintenance of their most vital asset – their health.

We can't live without a functioning stove or washing machine, and we attend to their maintenance promptly. However, when it comes to the most important machine on Earth – our body – we tend to procrastinate until we hit rock bottom and desperately search for a solution. The problem with this approach is that sometimes it becomes impossible to climb out of the hole we've dug for ourselves, potentially leading to pain, suffering, and even death, affecting not just ourselves but also our loved ones.

This self-destructive approach is a form of violence towards ourselves and those who care about us. Neglecting self-care not only leads to a diminished quality of life but also contradicts nature's intention for peace, balance, and creation. Self-neglect can take various forms, but one of the most common is avoiding the life we deserve by focusing on what we lack instead of appreciating what we have. We make excuses for why we can't have or achieve certain things, perpetuating the problem rather than seeking solutions.

Hitting rock bottom often involves a repertoire of excuses, with time and money being the most frequently used ones. To challenge these excuses, I conducted a social experiment at our center, offering donation-based Alphabiotic alignment services for five months. Despite extensive promotion of our donation-based Alphabiotic alignment services, the turnout was disappointingly low, highlighting a common reluctance to embracing one's own health and new health approaches. Regular attendees were asked why their relatives or neighbors didn't join them, and they provided various excuses like lack of time, absence of pain, disbelief in the effectiveness, skepticism towards alternative methods, transportation issues, and more.

Interestingly, when these excuses were no longer valid, as in the case of free transportation provided by a dedicated woman we called the "Ambulance," new excuses emerged. It became clear that even individuals suffering from pain and disease weren't always willing to seize an opportunity for relief. I encountered similar resistance when offering my services to individuals dealing with serious health conditions like brain cancer. Despite their dramatic and sad social media posts, they didn't respond positively to the offer, prioritizing other activities to numb their pain rather than exploring potential solutions.

The cost of neglecting our health is profound and multifaceted, extending far beyond mere financial implications. The price includes physical and emotional pain and suffering, affecting not only the individual but also their families, friends, and colleagues. It requires time spent in waiting rooms, undergoing medical tests, and relying on pharmaceutical interventions. However, the most significant cost is losing lives without realizing that better options exist.

Through Biomagnetism and my self-care book, *Biomagnetism: The Mind, Body, Spirit Recalibration System,* I aim to provide you with an opportunity to live a life of optimal health. Although these methods may require out-of-pocket expenses, the investment yields invaluable results – living a healthy, medicine-free life. Some may hesitate due to a narrow focus on financial concerns, but excluding these methods from the medical field perpetuates a costly and failing healthcare system.

Consider the financial burden of conventional treatments like chemotherapy, radiotherapy, and surgeries, which can amount to hundreds of thousands of dollars. In exchange for this hefty price, individuals often experience depleted quality of life, misery, and a false sense of hope. In contrast, Biomagnetism offers a more affordable and effective alternative, with numerous success stories and testimonials available for reference. By embracing these methods, we can revolutionize the healthcare system, making it more inclusive, cost-effective, and focused on genuine healing.

Excuses, serving as barriers to action, significantly contribute to our physical, emotional, and spiritual suffering. If we want to live life to the fullest, we must let go of excuses and embrace a system that allows us to thrive. This book provides you with the knowledge and tools to do so, free of charge. It's a compilation of over 20 years of study and experience, designed to help you unlock the secrets of a fulfilling life.

Many people live day to day without considering Biomagnetism or Alphabiotic alignments because they believe these methods are only for those who are broken and in pain. However, balance and well-being should be pursued by everyone, regardless of their current state. At our wellness center, we offer balance solutions for newborns and individuals in their final moments of life because healing and balance enhance the quality of life under any circumstances.

Hitting rock bottom can manifest in various ways, often through self-medication with substances like alcohol, drugs, or unhealthy behaviors. It's time to experience a natural high by adopting a lifestyle that incorporates this holistic system. I want to clarify that I'm not criticizing you, medical doctors, or the medical system.

There is a wealth of information and misunderstanding surrounding these subjects, but Goizean Biomagnetists witness scientific miracles every day. Many practitioners, including myself, have healed through Biomagnetism after exhausting countless other treatments and therapies. If hospitals genuinely aim to facilitate healing, they should incorporate biomagnetic therapists into their systems. However, this change won't happen spontaneously. It requires individuals like you, who are brave enough to embrace alternative approaches like Goizean Biomagnetism, to speak up and share their healing experiences, even in the face of ridicule.

I also encourage you to advocate for insurance coverage of these therapies. Submit claims and assert your right to access them. By planting these seeds of change in the collective consciousness, we can save more lives and alleviate unnecessary suffering. Now, the responsibility lies with you, as you hold this invaluable information in your hands.

There is no need to convince anyone forcefully that they can benefit from our solutions. As a biomagnetic therapist, I have witnessed thousands of individuals healing through this method when all hope seemed lost, even in cases of emotional blockages. As more people become aware of this biomagnetic solution, a decision will be made. Some will eagerly seize the opportunity, while others may resist, not fully realizing the potential benefits of utilizing nature's resources for their health.

Allow me to share a poignant and unfortunate story that taught me a profound lesson about the power of the mind and decision-making. I received a call from a woman, concerned about her 37-year-old friend diagnosed with leg cancer, seeking hope through Biomagnetism. After discussing Biomagnetism and its potential benefits, she expressed enthusiasm and promised to schedule an appointment for her friend. Shortly after speaking, she contacted me again frustrated because her friend didn't believe in the power of magnets to aid his health. Although she pleaded for me to intervene, I explained that I cannot impose myself on others, especially when they do not ask or desire my help. I also emphasized that once the gentleman started chemotherapy, it would be risky to engage in Biomagnetism alongside it.

A week later, the woman called again, informing me that her friend had a change of heart and now wanted to try Biomagnetism.

Unfortunately, by that point, the chemotherapy had taken a toll, and it was too late to pursue Biomagnetism safely. Tragically, the patient endured a harrowing six-month battle with cancer before passing away, leaving behind two young children.

While we may never fully comprehend the thought process behind such decisions, it's evident that people often surrender their power and entrust decision-making to others, sometimes at the cost of their lives. For instance, if a doctor declares that there is no cure for a health issue, will you accept this statement as an absolute truth without exploring alternative options like Biomagnetism and nutritional shifts? Similarly, if a physician dismisses Biomagnetism without proper training or knowledge, will you accept their advice unquestioningly?

It's crucial not to succumb to fear or make decisions solely based on fear. Fear clouds judgment and can lead us to accept harmful recommendations without considering other possibilities. Therefore, it's important to ask yourself if you're open to trying something new, even if it means challenging your beliefs and stepping out of your comfort zone.

This painful but enlightening lesson impacted the woman who initially sought Biomagnetism for her friend. After experiencing its benefits firsthand, she introduced other friends to the practice, enriching their lives. It serves as a reminder that problems can sometimes lead to positive outcomes.

Consider the story of Dr. Isaac Goiz Duran, the founder of Biomagnetism, whose own suffering and the loss of his mother to cancer motivated him to seek effective solutions. Despite his father being a medical doctor, he experienced the pain, suffering, and helplessness of being unable to help his mother despite his medical training. This is yet another example of how traumatic emotional experiences can spur us to make new and beneficial discoveries.

Lastly, I invite you to envision a world of justice, peace, and balance that starts within each individual. Picture a life where anger exists but violence is set aside, where genuine forgiveness is sought when harm is done. Imagine a life where we release harmful emotions by forgiving ourselves and others for past actions. Envision a life where sacrifice is replaced by the understanding that what we surrender yields far greater value.

Imagine a world where education endeavors are directed not just on skills acquisition but at cultivating abilities that foster peace, balance, and well-being in others. Picture a life where we communicate honestly and meaningfully, fostering strong relationships. Envision a world where envy and greed serve as temporary obstacles that lead us to recognize that our only competition is with ourselves, inspiring us to live our own authentic lives rather than comparing ourselves to others.

Imagine a life where we celebrate strengths rather than criticizing weaknesses. Lastly, imagine a life filled with love, gratitude, and appreciation for all that life offers. These simple ideas can bring about profound changes in our lives. Imagination is the starting point for all transformation. Dare to dream big and put those dreams into action. I invite you to embrace this way of thinking. The possibilities are boundless!

Chapter 19

Bonus Section: Pain-Dysfunction Harmonizer

Ａs a bonus to this book and insight into its sequel, *Biomagnetism: The Mind, Body, Spirit Recalibration System,* here is a highly effective pain/dysfunction harmonizing protocol. It's one of several to be featured in that book.

To secure health magnets to conduct this pain relief biomagnetic protocol on yourself, you can go to *www.SaveMeMagnets.com*.

The Pain-Dysfunction Harmonizer biomagnetic strategy has proven effective in alleviating and, in many cases, completely resolving pain. This method offers a safe and natural alternative to traditional pain relief approaches, such as addictive or potentially harmful painkillers.

Important Notice: It's noteworthy that some individuals have experienced a temporary increase in pain after applying this protocol. Interestingly, this is often a positive sign, indicative of the transformative process underway. These same individuals have subsequently reported a significant reduction or even complete disappearance of pain after continued application.

Reminder: While this biomagnetic combination can be highly effective, it should not be seen as a replacement for professional medical care. Always seek appropriate medical advice and treatment when needed. After receiving medical care, you can use this strategy as a complementary approach.

Suggested Usage – Application Timing (30 Minutes):

- Physical Trauma (Cuts, Sprains, Bruises, etc.), General Localized Pain, Tumor Growths: Apply once (or as desired) daily until the pain ceases.

- **Guiding Question:** What factors, spanning mind, body, and spirit, are contributing to this pain (challenge)? What actions or inactions might be influencing this discomfort?

Magnet Trio Placement:

1. **Target Area for Pain, Dysfunction, or Growth:** Apply a negative (−) magnet directly on the specific area experiencing pain, dysfunction, or abnormal growth. This could include regions such as the head for headaches, liver for conditions like cirrhosis, pancreas in cases of diabetes, stomach, site of a fracture, lymph nodes, tumors, moles, and other affected areas. The precise application of the negative magnet is designed to address the discomfort or disorder right at its source, facilitating targeted relief and supporting the body's natural healing processes.

2. **Left Kidney:** Place a positive (+) magnet here. Note that the left kidney is positioned slightly higher than right.

3. **Right Kidney:** Position a positive (+) magnet to this area.

(* Notice that left kidney is slightly higher than right kidney)

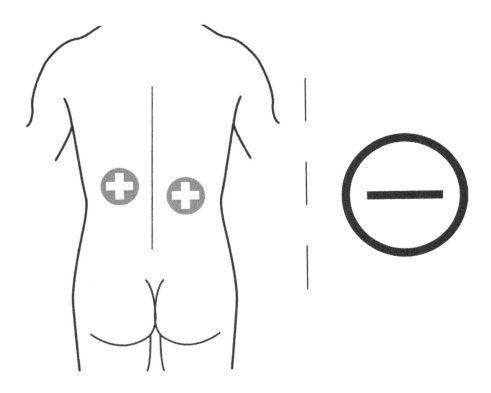

The End

Is A New Beginning

Take Responsibility for what you Create in your Life

About the Author:
Moses Durazo

Moses Durazo is a dedicated advocate for holistic medicine industries in the United States and internationally. Based in Santa Ana, California, he has spent years exploring and promoting natural medicine approaches to wellness and healing.

Durazo's journey into the world of alternative medicine began with his studies as a Medical Assistant at the University of California Irvine Medical Clinic. His passion for healthcare and academic research led him to the Center for AIDS Prevention Studies (CAPS) at the University of California San Francisco and Children's Hospital of Los Angeles, where he served as a research assistant.

During his undergraduate studies at the University of California Santa Cruz (UCSC), Durazo discovered the field of holistic healthcare, which sparked a paradigm shift in his thinking. He completed UCSC's holistic health practitioner certification program and earned a Bachelor of Arts in Language Studies. This combination of holistic medicine and language studies expanded his perspective and inspired him to explore the healing practices of different cultures.

Durazo's travels to Europe, Asia, and Latin America reinforced his belief in the universal need for optimal mind, body, and spiritual balance. He participated in a university summer-long work-abroad program in Switzerland, gaining valuable insights into the common struggles shared by people from diverse backgrounds.

In 2008, a trip to Mexico ignited Durazo's curiosity about Medical Pair Biomagnetism. He met a dentist who had witnessed remarkable healing and pain reduction through this biomagnetic science. Determined to study the theories of Dr. Isaac Goiz Durán, Durazo returned to Mexico City and became captivated by the transformative results of biomagnetic therapy.

Durazo's personal experience with chronic health issues further solidified his commitment to Biomagnetism. After finding his cure through biomagnetic therapy, he knew he had discovered his life's mission – to pioneer this science and bring its benefits to others.

In addition to his work in the medical biomagnetic field, Durazo is an advocate for multidimensional health and holistic training. He has trained in Alphabiotic (Spinal) Alignments, embracing a hands-on approach to well-being.

As a passionate educator, Durazo has developed on-demand courses to teach people the fundamentals of Recalibration Biomagnetism. He has also created self-care biomagnetic kits available on Amazon, empowering individuals to take control of their health and wellness.

Moses Durazo's books, including: *How Magnets Can Save Your Life, Dr. Goiz' Medical Biomagnetic Pair Therapy and Bioenergetics Made Easy, How to Cure with Alternative Medicine without Government Interference, Medical Magnets: Saving Lives and Millions of Dollars in Healthcare, Magnets to the Rescue, The Power of Self-Care – Using*

Biomagnetism for Suicide Prevention and Mental Wellness, and *Why You Need to Start Using Biomagnetism,* reflect his dedication to holistic health and his mission to share the transformative power of biomagnetic therapy with the world. Durazo continues to advocate for alternative healing approaches that prioritize optimal well-being for all.

Bibliography

Chang, Dr. Stephen T. The Tao of Sexology: The Book of Infinite Sex Wisdom. Reno, NV: Tao Publishing, 1986

Chang, Dr. Stephen T. The Tao of Balanced Diet. Reno, NV: Tao Publishing, 1979

Chang, Dr. Stephen T. The Complete System of Self-Healing Internal Exercises. Reno, NV: Tao Publishing, 1986

Collins, E. (2009). An a-z guide to healing foods. San Francisco, CA: Conari Press.

T. Colin Campbell, PhD & Thomas M. Campbell II, MD, The China Study. Bendella Books, Inc. (2006)

Rinn, R. C., & Carson, R. E. (2009). Harnessing the healing power of fruit. Lake Mary, FL: Siloam.

Copyright 2007-2011, Environmental Working Group http://www.ewg. org/water/downthedrain 14 August, 2011

Herd Immunity: Three Reasons Why I Don't Vaccinate My Children… And Why Vaccine Supporters Shouldn't Care That I Use Vaccine Exemption Forms By: Shane Ellison, MS

http://thepeopleschemist.com/reasons-dont-vaccinate-children-vaccine-supporters-shouldnt-give/April 16, 2013

Ingredients of Vaccines - Fact Sheet - CDC

http://www.cdc.gov/vaccines/vac-gen/additives.htmApril 18, 2013

The New Medicine of Dr Hamer, by Walter Last

http://customers.hbci.com/~wenonah/new/hamer.htm May 6, 2013

The Germanic/German New Medicine

http://www.newmedicine.ca/ May 6, 2013

Healthful Living

http://www.healthfullivingsd.com/joom/index.php/articles/119-the-healing-power-of-nutsDecember 10, 2013

Nourishing Interactive

http://www.nourishinteractive.com/healthy-living/free-nutrition-articles/121-list-seeds-nuts December 10, 2013

Everyday Health, Inc.

http://www.joybauer.com/food-articles/nuts-and-seeds.aspx#brazil December 10, 2013

Care2.com Inc.

http://www.care2.com/greenliving/5-super-health-benefits-of-sunflower-seeds.html December 10, 2013

Health Media Ventures Inc.

http://www.health.com/health/gallery/0,,20559953_2,00.html December 10, 2013

Coconut Secrets

http://www.coconutsecret.com/saturatedfats2.html January 12, 2014

https://thehighwire.com/ark-videos/aborted-fetal-tissue-in-vaccines/

https://thebiblesays.com/commentary/deut/deut-22/deuteronomy-229-12/

https://www.chop.edu/news/feature-article-fetal-cells-and-vaccines-common-questions-answered

https://mvec.mcri.edu.au/references/foetal-embryonic-cells-utilised-in-vaccine-development-platforms/

https://www.destinyimage.com/blog/2016/05/28/the-principle-of-spiritual-trading

https://crossexamined.org/abortion-and-the-god-molech/

https://mvec.mcri.edu.au/references/foetal-embryonic-cells-utilised-in-vaccine-development-platforms/

BMC Health Serv Res. 2012 Aug 1:12:231. doi: 10.1186/1472-6963-12-231. How healthcare professionals respond to parents with religious objections to vaccination: a qualitative study. Wilhelmina L M Ruijs 1 , Jeannine L A Hautvast, Giovanna van IJzendoorn, Wilke J C van Ansem, Glyn Elwyn, Koos van der Velden, Marlies E J L Hulscher https://pubmed.ncbi.nlm.nih.gov/22852838/

https://www.ncbi.nlm.nih.gov/pmc/articles/PMC2474726/

https://thehighwire.com/editorial/with-reckless-fda-approval-in-1998-sucralose-breaks-down-dna/

https://www.theepochtimes.com/health/top-covid-events-of-the-year-reveal-facts-unspoken-and-unknown-5551693 and https://osf.io/preprints/osf/b9t7m

Dr. Thompson has been a scientist at CDC for nearly two generations and a senior scientist on over a dozen CDC publications at the core of many of CDC's vaccine safety claims. https://www.ncbi.nlm.nih.gov/pubmed

https://oig.hhs.gov/oei/reports/oei-04-07-00260.pdf (Splicing down this 58% of unidentified conflicts, 40% involved employment or grants, 13% involved equity ownership, and 5% involved consulting.)

https://www.nap.edu/read/1815/chapter/2#7

https://www.nap.edu/read/2138/chapter/2#12

https://www.nap.edu/read/13164/chapter/2#3

https://www.nap.edu/read/2138/chapter/12#307. See also https://www.nap.edu/read/1815/chapter/9

https://www.ncbi.nlm.nih.gov/books/NBK230053/ (HHS's 2014 review also added the following vaccine-injury pairs to the list of what it asserts are the most commonly claimed vaccine injuries: spontaneous abortion from HPV vaccine and meningitis from MMR vaccine.)

https://www.ncbi.nlm.nih.gov/books/NBK230053/

https://www.ncbi.nlm.nih.gov/books/NBK230053/

https://www.ncbi.nlm.nih.gov/books/NBK230053/

https://www.ncbi.nlm.nih.gov/books/NBK230053/

https://www.ncbi.nlm.nih.gov/pmc/articles/PMC3404712/ 242

https://www.ncbi.nlm.nih.gov/pmc/articles/PMC3404712/

https://www.ncbi.nlm.nih.gov/pmc/articles/PMC3404712/

https://www.ncbi.nlm.nih.gov/pmc/articles/PMC3404712/

https://www.ncbi.nlm.nih.gov/pmc/articles/PMC3404712/

https://www.ncbi.nlm.nih.gov/pubmed/23432812

https://www.ncbi.nlm.nih.gov/pubmed/23432812

The rotavirus vaccine is given orally, not injection, and hence not considered. Nonetheless, the 35 rotavirus studies HHS states compare "vaccinated with unvaccinated children" actually compare children receiving oral drops of rotavirus with children receiving oral drops of the following vaccine ingredients: Polysorbate 80, Sucrose, Citrate, Phosphate, Dextran, Sorbitol, Amino acids, Dulbecco's Modified Eagle Medium, Calcium Carbonate, and/or Xanthan. https://www.ncbi.nlm.nih.gov/books/NBK230057/table/results.t19/?report=objectonly

https://www.ncbi.nlm.nih.gov/books/NBK230053/

https://www.ncbi.nlm.nih.gov/books/NBK230053/

https://slate.com/health-and-science/2017/12/flaws-in-the-clinical-trials-for-gardasil-made-it-harder-to-properly-assess-safety.html

https://slate.com/health-and-science/2017/12/flaws-in-the-clinical-trials-for-gardasil-made-it-harder-to-properly-assess-safety.html

https://slate.com/health-and-science/2017/12/flaws-in-the-clinical-trials-for-gardasil-made-it-harder-to-properly-assess-safety.html

https://slate.com/health-and-science/2017/12/flaws-in-the-clinical-trials-for-gardasil-made-it-harder-to-properly-assess-safety.html

https://slate.com/health-and-science/2017/12/flaws-in-the-clinical-trials-for-gardasil-made-it-harder-to-properly-assess-safety.html

http://bioethics.hms.harvard.edu/person/faculty-members/marcia-angell

https://www.nybooks.com/articles/2009/01/15/drug-companies-doctorsa-story-of-corruption/

https://www.ncbi.nlm.nih.gov/pmc/articles/PMC7293525/ A newborn's brain development will not be complete until early adulthood.

https://www.ncbi.nlm.nih.gov/pmc/articles/PMC3722610/

https://web.archive.org/web/20170723025206/http://www.fda.gov/downloads/BiologicsBloodVaccines/Vaccines/ApprovedProducts/UCM244522.pdf

https://web.archive.org/web/20170723025206/http://www.fda.gov/downloads/BiologicsBloodVaccines/Vaccines/ApprovedProducts/UCM244522.pdf

https://web.archive.org/web/20170723025206/http://www.fda.gov/downloads/BiologicsBloodVaccines/Vaccines/ApprovedProducts/UCM244522.pdf

https://web.archive.org/web/20170723025206/http://www.fda.gov/downloads/BiologicsBloodVaccines/Vaccines/ApprovedProducts/UCM244522.pdf

Both Rotavirus vaccines are given via oral drop and hence not discussed. Nonetheless, RotaTeq (Merck)'s "placebo" contained Polysorbate 80, Sucrose, Citrate and Phosphate, and Rotarix (GSK)'s "placebo" contained Sucrose, Dextran, Sorbitol, Amino acids, Dulbecco's Modified Eagle Medium, Calcium Carbonate, and Xanthan.

https://www.fda.gov/downloads/BiologicsBloodVaccines/Vaccines/ApprovedProducts/ UCM133539.pdf

https://www.fda.gov/downloads/BiologicsBloodVaccines/Vaccines/ApprovedProducts/UCM142288.pdf

https://www.accessdata.fda.gov/drugsatfda_docs/label/2011/103000s5236lbl.pdf

https://www.accessdata.fda.gov/drugsatfda_docs/label/2011/018936s091lbl.pdf

https://www.accessdata.fda.gov/drugsatfda_docs/label/2009/020702s056lbl.pdf

Both Rotavirus vaccines are given via oral drop and hence not discussed. Nonetheless, RotaTeq (Merck)'s "placebo" contained Polysorbate 80, Sucrose, Citrate and Phosphate, and Rotarix (GSK)'s "placebo" contained Sucrose, Dextran, Sorbitol, Amino acids, Dulbecco's Modified Eagle Medium, Calcium Carbonate, and Xanthan.

https://www.fda.gov/downloads/BiologicsBloodVaccines/Vaccines/ApprovedProducts/ UCM133539.pdf

https://www.fda.gov/downloads/BiologicsBloodVaccines/Vaccines/ApprovedProducts/UCM142288.pdf

https://www.wiley.com/en-us/Vaccines+and+Autoimmunity-p-9781118663431

https://www.ncbi.nlm.nih.gov/pubmed/25923134

https://www.fda.gov/downloads/biologicsbloodvaccines/vaccines/approvedproducts/ucm111263.pdf

https://www.fda.gov/downloads/biologicsbloodvaccines/vaccines/approvedproducts/ucm111263.pdf

https://www.clinicaltrials.gov/ct2/show/results/NCT00092547?term=nct+00092547&rank=1&sect=X430156&view=results

https://www.fda.gov/downloads/biologicsbloodvaccines/vaccines/approvedproducts/ucm111263.pdf

https://www.wiley.com/en-us/Vaccines+and+Autoimmunity-p-9781118663431

This defective clinical trial design may have been influenced by the HHS agency and its employees that developed the patent used to develop Gardasil and receive royalties from its sale.

https://www.ott.nih.gov/news/nih-technology-licensed-merck-hpv-vaccine

https://www.cdc.gov/vaccines/pubs/pinkbook/downloads/appendices/B/us-vaccines.pdf

https://www.fda.gov/downloads/BiologicsBloodVaccines/Vaccines/ApprovedProducts/UCM110049.pdf

(The "Placebo (Alum Diluent)" contained 300µg AAHS and thimerosal, https://www.nejm.org/doi/full/10.1056/NEJM199208133270702)

http://www.oatext.com/pdf/JTS-3-187.pdf

https://healthit.ahrq.gov/sites/default/files/docs/publication/r18hs017045-lazarus-final-report-2011.pdf

https://wonder.cdc.gov/vaers.html

SaveMeMagnets.com

We invite you to stay connected. Follow us on social media. Our handle is *@SaveMeMagnets* on:

- X
- Instagram
- Facebook
- LinkedIn
- YouTube

Also, want to help inform your loved ones about the wonderful world of Biomagnetism?

Download our free eBook at:
www.OurWellnessToday.com

Made in the USA
Monee, IL
26 June 2024

60551785R00100